Internal control and accounting project

Michael Fardon

Published by Osborne Books Limited
Unit 1B Everoak Estate
Bromyard Road, Worcester WR2 5HP
Tel 01905 748071
Email books@osbornebooks.co.uk
Website www.osbornebooks.co.uk

Design by Laura Ingham

Printed by CPI Group (UK) Limited, Croydon, CRO 4YY, on environmentally friendly, acid-free paper from managed forests.

British Library Cataloguing in Publication Data
A catalogue record for this book is available from the British Library

ISBN 978 1909173 316

Contents

Acknowledgements

The author wishes to thank Jon Moore and Cathy Turner for their help with the production of this book. The author is also grateful to Jo Osborne and Roger Petheram for contributing practical ideas and advice about the delivery of the course. Thanks are also due to to Bethan Nevin for her technical editing and to Laura Ingham for her designs for this series.

The publisher is indebted to the Association of Accounting Technicians for its help and advice to our authors and editors during the preparation of this text and for its permission to reproduce the Sample Assessment included in this book. Thanks are also due to Marks & Spencer Group plc and Tesco plc for reproduction of extracts from their CSR documentation.

Author

Michael Fardon has extensive teaching experience of a wide range of banking, business and accountancy courses at Worcester College of Technology. He now specialises in writing business and financial texts and is General Editor at Osborne Books. He is also an educational consultant and has worked extensively in the areas of vocational business curriculum development.

Introduction

what this book covers

This book has been written specifically to cover the 'Internal control and accounting systems' Unit which is mandatory for the revised (2013) AAT Level 4 Diploma in Accounting.

This book is different from other Osborne Books AAT Tutorials in that it is more of a handbook for the Unit rather than a series of traditional chapters with activities.

It is based on the situation that the student has a choice of two assessment methods:

- writing a report based on workplace evidence
- writing a report based on an AAT Case Study

These two assessment methods have a number of requirements in common which are covered by a sequence of separate chapters in the book. These common requirements are:

- learning about the the theoretical aspects of organisations, accounting systems, legislation, regulations, fraud, professional ethics and sustainability
- analysing and reviewing an accounting system
- writing a formal report

The book also contains example material for both assessment routes in the form of a sample Case Study produced by the AAT and reproduced here with their kind permission.

1 Introduction to internal control and accounting systems

this chapter covers...

This first chapter is an introduction to the Unit 'Internal control and accounting systems.'
The chapter will explain:

■ *the reasons why this Unit is rather different from any other you will have encountered so far in your studies*

■ *the two possible assessment methods – using workplace evidence or a written Case Study – and what they involve*

■ *what will be expected of you as you complete the Unit*

■ *how to organise your method of working to make the most of your resources – and especially your time*

■ *the need to map the assessment criteria, illustrated with an AAT sample Mapping Document*

INTRODUCTION TO THE 'PROJECT' UNIT

what this Unit involves

The Unit 'Internal control and accounting systems' combines six AAT Learning Outcomes which will be assessed in an extended project:

- understand the role of accounting within the organisation
- understand the importance and use of internal control systems
- evaluate the accounting system and identify areas for improvement
- conduct an ethical evaluation of the accounting system
- conduct a sustainability evaluation of the accounting system
- make recommendations to improve the accounting system

what you will learn

When you have completed this Unit you should be able to:

- **understand the role of accounting** in an organisation in supporting different departments of the organisation and dealing with outside organisations and individuals
- understand the importance and principles of **internal control** of the accounting function in an organisation – to help efficiency and to identify potential fraud and breaches of professional ethics
- **evaluate an accounting system** in a real-life situation or in an AAT Case Study by:
    - identifying the requirements of the accounting system
    - working out the improvements that could be made
    - making suggestions as to how the improvements could be implemented
    - identifying the impact that the changes would make on the system and its users

your assessment – the Report

The assessment takes the form of a **formal Report** (4,000 to 5,000 words) submitted electronically to AAT for marking by your training provider, who will be required to ensure that all areas for assessment have been covered.

This Report can be based on:

- your findings from an actual **workplace,** or
- an AAT **Case Study**

Your tutor will be able to advise you on which option to take – workplace evidence or Case Study.

Whatever you decide to do, you will find that this is where this Unit differs in its assessment from most of the other assessments you will have encountered so far in your studies. It is not difficult, but it is challenging and it is different.

You will find that your studies will give you the opportunity to take on a new role – almost that of a consultant – and you can be creative in your approach and thinking. The content of your Report should:

- **review a current accounting system**, focusing on record keeping systems, principles of internal control, methods of fraud prevention, and issues relating to professional ethics and sustainability

- **analyse a current accounting system**, identifying weaknesses or areas where improvement could be made and making recommendations to improve the system, bearing in mind all the costs involved

WHAT YOU WILL NEED TO DO – AN OVERVIEW

This section is intended to give you an idea of what you need to do in order to write your Report. It is not exhaustive and you are recommended to discuss these requirements with your tutor.

initial research and setting the scene

To start with, you should:

- give a **description of the organisation**, which could be a real workplace or based on a Case Study

- define the structure, purpose and organisation of the **accounting function** within the overall organisation

- identify the **relationship** between the accounting function and the other internal departments

- identify the important **external relationships** the organisation maintains; this could include relationships with customers, suppliers, shareholders, banks, trade organisations and governmental bodies such as HM Revenue & Customs

- decide **what an organisation requires from its accounting systems** – these requirements will differ depending on the nature and size of the organisation and will often be based on computer software solutions

review of the accounting system

You will then need to **review the accounting system** to ensure that it meets the requirements of the organisation. In short . . .

- how good is it?
- do things go wrong?
- could things go wrong?

This review involves:

■ deciding **which areas of the accounting system you will evaluate** – including, for example, sales, purchases, credit control, banking, payroll, petty cash, budgeting and management reporting; if it is a small organisation with a simple structure you could cover a number of these; if it is a larger, more complex, organisation, just one or two areas may be evaluated

■ identifying the **strengths and weaknesses** of the accounting system this should include a review of the working methods used within the accounting system to ensure that the best results are being achieved especially in terms of cost-effectiveness, reliability and speed

■ describing the **external regulations** that will influence the way the accounting system will operate (eg legislation affecting payroll, or VAT regulations)

■ **reviewing and evaluating the internal control system** by identifying areas where there is a potential for **error**

■ **reviewing and evaluating the internal control system** by identifying areas where there is a potential for **fraud** involving loss of money, inventory or working time, and then assessing the level of risk of that fraud – ie how likely it is

■ identifying **ways of detecting fraud** and the types of **internal controls** that could be established to prevent fraud occurring

■ identifying breaches or threats to the fundamental principles of **professional ethics**, eg petty theft in the workplace

■ assessing the extent to which the accounting system fulfils the requirements of **sustainability** principles (eg by recycling resources, saving energy and by encouraging cycling to work)

■ **reviewing the weaknesses** that have been identified in the accounting system and explaining their impact upon the organisation – in terms of time, money and reputation (for example the loss of revenue, time wasting, letting customers down)

making recommendations

You will need to be able to make clear and sensible recommendations to rectify the weaknesses identified in the evaluation of the accounting systems:

- for every weakness identified you must make **at least one recommendation** for improvement
- if you have identified just **one weakness** within an accounting system then you should compare **two or three possible solutions** and state, with reasons, which solution you believe to be the best
- you should work out the **comparative cost** of the recommendations you are making, for example the cost of training, new computers, and the benefits they will provide; the need for staff training is very important

THE LEARNING PROCESS IN THIS BOOK

The processes described so far – and the thought of writing a report – may seem scary, but when you have finished this chapter you should be much more familiar with what is required and see how it all fits together.

There are three processes involved –- the three 'R's:

1	**R**esearch the workplace or **R**ead the Case Study
2	**R**eview the accounting system and make recommendations
3	**R**eport writing - learning about structure and style

1   **research and read – learning the theory**

In order to be able to assess an organisation and its accounting system you will need to acquire basic knowledge about areas such as:

- types of organisation – their needs and links with the commercial world
- accounting systems – their areas of activity and how they link with the rest of the organisation
- internal control systems
- the dangers of fraud and the levels of risk involved
- the requirements of the AAT Code of Professional Ethics
- the need for sustainability and practical ways of achieving it
- cost-benefit analysis – how to assess the benefits of a recommendation in relation to its costs

All these theoretical areas are covered in the chapters that immediately follow this one. These are:

Chapter 2   **Organisations and accounting systems**

This explains the way in which accounting systems work and how they support the organisation and how they relate to outside bodies.

Chapter 3   **Internal control systems and fraud**

This explains the way in which an organisation and its accounting system should exercise control over its operations and so avoid fraud.

Chapter 4   **Professional ethics and sustainability**

This explains the way in which an organisation and its accounting system can be evaluated in terms of ethics and policies which promote 'sustainability'.

2   **review the system and make recommendations**

When you are confident of your knowledge in these areas, you will be able to:

■ **review** an accounting system

■ make **recommendations** for improvement

■ assess the benefits of a recommendation in relation to its **costs**

This is covered in:

Chapter 5   **Reviewing systems and making recommendations**

This will explain how you can review and evaluate an accounting system and carry out a cost-benefit analysis – assessing the benefits of each recommendation in relation to its costs.

3   **report**

At this stage you will be ready to write your Report. This is covered in

Chapter 6   **Writing the Report**

This will explain all you need to know about structuring and writing the text of a formal report.

As noted earlier this report can be based on:

■ your findings from an actual **workplace,** or

■ an AAT **Case Study**

In order to show you what is required by these two forms of assessment we include AAT sample assessment material at the end of this book.

THE REPORT

The basis of your assessment is a Report of 4,000 to 5,000 words, often referred to as 'The Project', which has to be submitted online as a Computer-Based Project to your assessor, and which must cover all the **AAT Assessment Criteria** set out on pages 12 to 13.

The diagram on the opposite page shows you the processes that you will normally go through to produce your **workplace evidence** – to complete the Report. Please study it carefully and then read the notes that follow. If you are using an **AAT Case Study** instead of workplace evidence, the processes will be similar. Whichever route you take to complete the Project you will have **a limit of six months** for completion and submission of the Report for formal assessment after teaching has finished. This includes a period of **two months** available for resubmitting the Report if additional evidence is required or other changes are recommended. A maximum of **four resubmissions** is allowed over these two months.

It is our aim in this book to make the writing of this Report as smooth and painless as possible. In most cases you will have people to help you both at your training provider and also at your workplace (if you have one), and you also have this text to fill in the gaps in your theoretical knowledge.

finding a 'workplace' or using an AAT Case Study

One of the most difficult parts of preparing for the Report is making initial decisions. You will have to decide what organisation (if any) you are going to use as a basis for your Report and what areas of the organisation you are going to write about. If you are working in an organisation or do voluntary work you will be able to gather **workplace evidence**. If you are an accounts manager or working in an accounts department, life is made easy for you, but if you are currently not working and are studying to get a qualification to enable you to work, this option may not be open to you. All workplace evidence that you provide must be:

- **valid** – it must be relevant to your investigation
- **authentic** – it must be real
- **current** – it must relate to current practice
- **sufficient** – there must be enough of it

If you find that there is not enough scope in your chosen organisation to provide all the evidence you need, your assessor will ask you to explain about the missing Assessment Criteria in an Appendix to the Report.

As noted above, if you do not work in an accounting environment, or at all, you may wish to take advantage of the **AAT Case Study** assessment method.

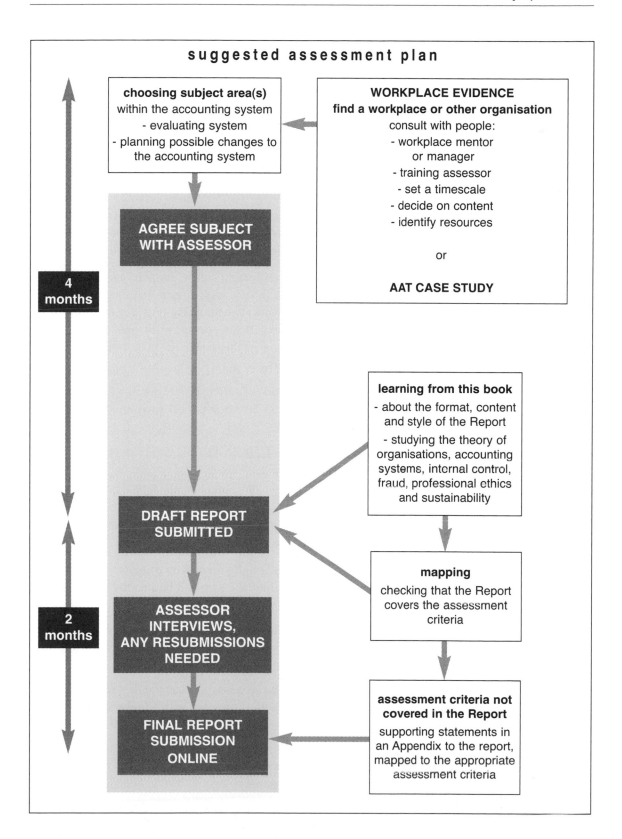

suggested assessment plan

choosing subject area(s)
within the accounting system
- evaluating system
- planning possible changes to
the accounting system

WORKPLACE EVIDENCE
find a workplace or other organisation
consult with people:
- workplace mentor
or manager
- training assessor
- set a timescale
- decide on content
- identify resources

or

AAT CASE STUDY

**AGREE SUBJECT
WITH ASSESSOR**

**4
months**

learning from this book
- about the format, content
and style of the Report

- studying the theory of
organisations, accounting
systems, internal control,
fraud, professional ethics
and sustainability

**DRAFT REPORT
SUBMITTED**

mapping
checking that the Report
covers the assessment
criteria

**ASSESSOR
INTERVIEWS,
ANY RESUBMISSIONS
NEEDED**

**2
months**

**assessment criteria not
covered in the Report**
supporting statements in
an Appendix to the report,
mapped to the appropriate
assessment criteria

**FINAL REPORT
SUBMISSION
ONLINE**

choosing a subject

The next decision to be made is the subject of your Report. You will need to find an area in an accounting environment – eg payroll processing, paying suppliers, cash handling – which could be improved so that its processes become more efficient and less open to error and fraud.

You will also need to relate this area of activity to issues involving professional ethics and sustainability (eg recycling of materials, car sharing to save fuel and reducing atmospheric pollution).

Note that if the organisation you choose is a large one, you can choose just one area of the accounting system. If the organisation is much smaller you may need to choose more than one accounting area for investigation.

If you are in work, this identification of a suitable area should be straightforward, as you will have time to look around and make the most of what you see. If you are not in work, your training provider may be able to arrange for you to do work experience or to work shadow. Time for investigation will be more limited in this case, but you should be able to decide on a subject for the Report.

If you are not in work, or if work experience or work shadowing are not possible, you should then identify an organisation such as a club or local charity which will be able to help.

If none of these options is available, the AAT Case Study should provide the evidence you need.

consulting with people – your mentor and assessor

It is important that, if you are in employment, you establish a relationship with a **mentor** (advisor) in the workplace who will be able to help you gather evidence and who will eventually be able to certify your work.

This mentor might be a line manager or a more senior manager. If you are not in work, you will have to find someone who is. This person will then become your 'mentor' and source of information.

You will also need to identify your **assessor** at your training provider. He or she should provide you with support, discussing with you the subject of your Report and monitoring its progress as you compile the evidence.

Whatever subject you choose, it should be agreed both with your employer or contact and also your assessor (eg your college tutor).

learning from this book

In order to make the most of this textbook, you should:

- start by reading Chapters 2, 3 and 4 which will provide you with the theoretical background for your investigations

- then read Chapter 5, which will explain how you can review and evaluate an accounting system and carry out a cost-benefit analysis – assessing the benefits of each recommendation in relation to its costs

- study Chapter 6 which will explain about the format of the Report, help you to choose the subject to be covered and make sure that you understand the assessment criteria that have to be covered

or, if you are taking the Case Study route . . .

- study the sample AAT Case Study and analyse the simulated workplace evidence which it will contain

time schedule

The diagram on page 9 proposes a plan for the writing and the assessment of the Report which should be completed within six months.

The Report will be submitted online and assessed by your training provider.

Note that AAT allows an initial four months for the writing and electronic submission of the Report and a further two months for any resubmissions, ie a total of six months.

MAPPING OF ASSESSMENT CRITERIA

An important part of the assessment process is the coverage of the **Unit assessment criteria** ie, what you have to cover. These are set out on the next two pages, together with page references to where they are covered in this book.

In your Report you will need to **map the assessment criteria** covered, ie give paragraph references to where the evidence is presented in your Report. You should refer to your tutor for the method you adopt for this. A sample AAT mapping document is shown on pages 14 and 15.

The important requirement of your assessment is that you should cover **all** the assessment criteria. It may be that this will not be possible in your Report, because of the workplace you have chosen to provide the evidence. This is not a problem: these 'missing' assessment criteria should be covered in full with supporting statements in the Appendix of the Report, mapped to the relevant assessment criteria. Your tutor will be able to advise about this.

INTERNAL CONTROL AND ACCOUNTING SYSTEMS: ASSESSMENT CRITERIA

Note: the numbers in brackets refer to the page numbers in this book.

Learning outcome 1

Understand the role of accounting within an organisation

1.1   Describe the purpose, structure and organisation of the accounting function and its relationships with other functions within the organisation. (20-22)

1.2   Explain the various business purposes for which the following financial information is required. (28-29)
- Statement of profit or loss
- Statement of cash flow
- Statement of financial position

1.3   Give an overview of the organisation's business and its critical external relationships with stakeholders. (18-19)

1.4   Explain how the accounting systems are affected by the organisational structure, systems, procedures, and business transactions. (20-24)

1.5   Explain the effect on users of changes to accounting systems caused by:
- External regulations (35-36)
- Organisational policies and procedures (36-38)

Learning outcome 2

Understand the importance and use of internal control systems

2.1   Identify the external regulations that affect accounting practice. (35-36)

2.2   Describe the causes of, and common types of, fraud and the impact of this on the organisation. (38-46)

2.3   Explain methods that can be used to detect fraud within an accounting system. (47-48)

2.4   Explain the types of controls that can be put in place to ensure compliance with statutory or organisational requirements. (35-36)

2.5   Explain how an internal control system can support the accounting function. (43-44)

Learning outcome 3

Evaluate the accounting system and identify areas for improvement

3.1   Identify an organisation's accounting system requirements including hardware and software packages. (69)

3.2   Review record keeping systems to confirm whether they meet the organisation's requirements. (68)

3.3   Identify weaknesses in and the potential for improvements to, the accounting system and consider their impact on the operation of the organisation. (69-70)

3.4   Identify potential areas of fraud arising from lack of control within the accounting system and evaluate the risk. (43-47)

3.5   Review methods of operating for cost effectiveness, reliability and speed. (68-69, 76-77)

Learning outcome 4

Conduct an ethical evaluation of the accounting systems

4.1   Evaluate the accounting system against ethical principles. (53-58)

4.2   Identify actual or possible breaches of professional ethics. (53-58)

Learning outcome 5

Conduct a sustainability evaluation of the accounting system

5.1   Evaluate the accounting system against sustainable principles. (59-62)

5.2   Identify where improvements could be made to improve sustainability. (59-62)

Learning outcome 6

Make recommendations to improve the accounting system

6.1   Make recommendations for changes to the accounting system, including ethical and sustainability considerations, with a clear rationale and an explanation of any assumptions made. (67-73)

6.2   Identify the effects that any recommended changes would have on the users of the system. (75)

6.3   Enable individuals to understand how to use the accounting system by use of: (75)
   • Training
   • Manuals
   • Written information
   • Help menus

6.4   Identify the implications of recommended changes in terms of time, financial costs, benefits, and operating procedures. (76-78)

AAT Mapping Document

Ref	Assessment criteria	Paragraph number	Assessor's comments
1.	**Understand the role of accounting within an organisation**		
1.1	Describe the purpose, structure and organisation of the accounting function and its relationship with other functions within the organisation		
1.2	Explain the various business purposes for which the following financial information is required – statement of profit or loss, statement of cash flow, and statement of financial position.		
1.3	Give an overview of the organisation's business and its critical external relationships with stakeholders.		
1.4	Explain how the accounting systems are affected by the organisational structure, systems, procedures and business transactions.		
1.5	Explain the effect on users of changes to accounting systems caused by external regulations, and organisational policies and procedures.		
2.	**Understand the importance and use of internal controls**		
2.1	Identify the external regulations that affect accounting practices.		
2.2	Describe the causes of and common types of fraud and the impact of this on the organisation.		
2.3	Explain the methods that can be used to detect fraud within an accounting system.		
2.4	Explain the types of controls that can be put in place to ensure compliance with statutory or organisational requirements.		
2.5	Explain how an internal control system can support the accounting function.		
3.	**Evaluate the accounting system and identify areas for improvement**		
3.1	Identify an organisation's accounting system, including hardware and software packages.		
3.2	Review record keeping systems to confirm whether they meet organisational requirement.		
3.3	Identify weaknesses in and the potential for improvements to the accounting system and consider their impact on the operation of the organisation.		
3.4	Identify potential areas of fraud arising from lack of control within the accounting system and evaluate the risk.		

Ref	Assessment criteria	Paragraph number	Assessor's comments
3.5	Review methods of operating for cost effectiveness, reliability and speed.		
4	**Conduct an ethical evaluation of the accounting system**		
4.1	Evaluate the accounting system against ethical principles.		
4.2	Identify actual or possible breaches of professional ethics.		
5	**Conduct a sustainability evaluation of the accounting system**		
5.1	Evaluate the accounting system against sustainable principles.		
5.2	Identify where improvements could be made to improve sustainability.		
6	**Make recommendations to improve the accounting system**		
6.1	Make recommendations for changes to the accounting system, including ethical and sustainability considerations with a clear rationale and an explanation of any assumptions made.		
6.2	Identify the effects that any changes would have on the users of the system.		
6.3	Enable individuals to understand how to use the accounting system by use of training, manuals, written information or help menus.		
6.4	Identify the implications of recommended changes in terms of time, financial costs, benefits and operating procedures.		

2 Organisations and accounting systems

this chapter covers...

In this chapter we examine the way in which the accounting function 'fits into' the overall structure of the organisation and how it relates to other organisations.

The areas the chapter covers include:

■ *the way in which what an organisation does – ie its 'business' – affects its accounting function*

■ *the influence of the external stakeholders of the organisation*

■ *the overall structure of the organisation*

■ *the structure of the accounting system*

■ *the way in which the accounting system interacts with the other functions*

■ *the administrative systems and control of resources within the organisation*

■ *the uses of the financial statements of the organisation*

■ *the effect on an accounting system of changes brought about by external regulations and internal policies and procedures*

You will see from these topics that this material forms much of what should go into the introductory and analysis sections of your Report.

Project writing hints are provided within the text of the Chapter.

THE 'BUSINESS' OF THE ORGANISATION

public and private sectors

Organisations are normally classed as public sector or private sector.

Public sector organisations are those owned or controlled directly or indirectly by the state. They include corporations like the BBC, Government Departments and local authorities. Their function is largely to provide some form of service: broadcasting, health, education, policing, refuse collection, tax collection, for example. Some public sector organisations form partnerships with private sector companies to provide a service, eg hospitals in the National Health Service.

Private sector organisations, on the other hand, are in private ownership, and include businesses ranging from the sole trader to the public limited company. The function of these organisations is to provide a product such as a car or TV or a service such as a holiday or a foot massage.

The range of activities carried out by both public and private sector organisations – the nature of their 'business' can therefore be classified as:

- providing goods – either through manufacturing or through retailing
- providing a service – either for consumers (private sector) or as a social benefit (public sector)

You may not consider that tax collection is a social benefit, but if you appreciate that tax revenue is used for Government spending on health and education, you will see the logic.

how the 'business' affects the accounting system

All organisations need accounting systems to carry out the accounting function. This function includes:

- processing and recording financial transactions – keeping accounts
- payroll
- costing and budgeting
- raising finance

You will see from this list that these are 'generic' functions which are common to all organisations. The variation is in the detail and will depend on the type of 'business' the organisation carries out:

- a manufacturing company in the private sector, for example, will keep accounts for suppliers and customers, will run payroll and will cost and budget for the manufacturing process and other activities; it is likely to raise finance from banks and possibly the equity markets

■ a local authority in the public sector will keep accounts for suppliers and to a lesser extent for customers, it will run payroll and keep to strict budgets; its financing, however, will come from Central Government, local enterprises and from local taxation

---

Report writing hint

When you write about the accounting system of your chosen organisation you will need to relate the system's functions to the type of activity carried out by the organisation – its 'business'.

DEALING WITH EXTERNAL STAKEHOLDERS

A stakeholder is a person or organisation that has an 'interest' in another organisation.

Stakeholders can be **internal** (eg employees, managers) or **external** (eg shareholders, banks, customers, suppliers, the tax authorities). Your assessment requirement covers the relationship with the **external stakeholders** of an organisation.

Take for example a retail organisation such as an electrical supermarket chain which is also a public limited company quoted on the stockmarket.

The functioning of the accounting system will be affected by external stakeholders in a number of ways:

■ **customers** will need to be provided with easy and efficient means of making payment, and in suitable circumstances, credit terms and finance

■ **suppliers** will need to be paid on time and credit terms and discounts will need to be negotiated and administered

■ **banks** that are lending money to the company are likely to require regular (eg monthly) management accounts, eg levels of sales, inventory, cash held, payables, receivables

■ the **tax authorities** (HM Revenue & Customs – a Government Department) will require calculation and payment of Corporation Tax, Value Added Tax and collection of Income Tax and National Insurance through the PAYE system

■ **shareholders** will require information about the financial performance of the company in the form of an annual financial report in paper format or downloadable from the company's website

- **trade associations** will request financial statistics such as sales trends, details of exports, wage rates and so on for their regular trade reports

The relationship of an organisation with its internal and external stakeholders is shown in the diagram set out below.

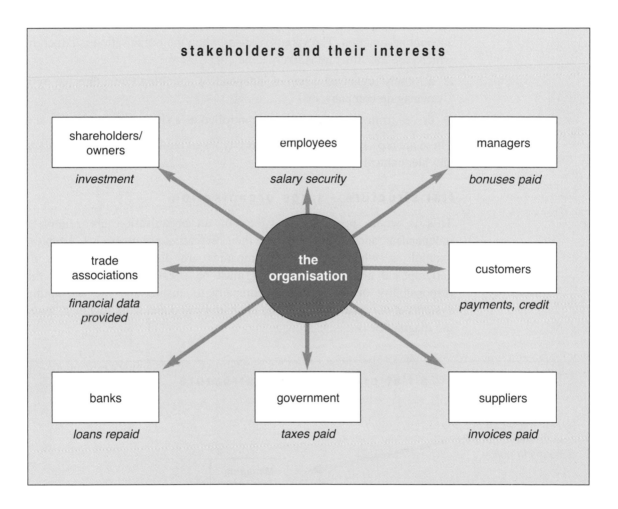

stakeholders and their interests

shareholders/owners
investment

employees
salary security

managers
bonuses paid

trade associations
financial data provided

the organisation

customers
payments, credit

banks
loans repaid

government
taxes paid

suppliers
invoices paid

Report writing hint

When you write about the accounting system of your chosen organisation you will need to identify external stakeholders who place demands on the activities of the accounting system and who affect financial decisions.

ORGANISATIONAL STRUCTURE

The organisation of the accounting system will depend a great deal on the way in which the organisation as a whole is structured.

In the case of a smaller organisation such as a private company the structure will be based on the shareholder directors being in charge of the whole business, with possibly a finance director in charge of the finance and accounting function. The variation arises when the organisation is larger, in which case the structure is likely to be either

- a loosely organised group of independent operating units, directed by a managing company, or
- driven from the top and tightly controlled as a single unit

These are represented by the two basic types of organisational structure: flat and hierarchical.

flat structure – large organisation

This is where operating divisions of an organisation are relatively independent, and are likely to have their own accounting systems. A typical example is where groups of companies are divided up in terms of geographical areas or products. It must be stressed that it will be the responsibility of the managing company to ensure that the accounting systems of the separate companies are harmonised and work together. Study the diagram below.

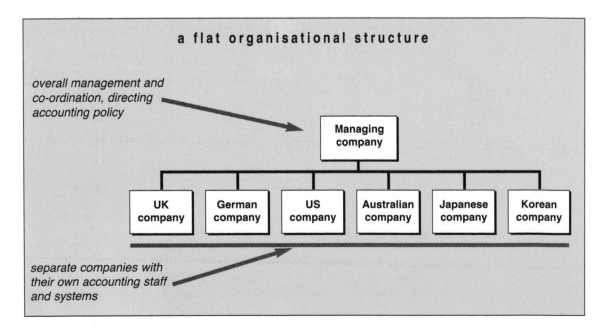

a flat organisational structure

overall management and co-ordination, directing accounting policy

Managing company

UK company | German company | US company | Australian company | Japanese company | Korean company

separate companies with their own accounting staff and systems

hierarchical structure – large organisation

A hierarchy is a series of levels of people, each level controlled by the level above it. This structure – also known as a 'tall' structure – is suitable for a large organisation such as a public limited company or Government Department which may have thousands of employees. In this type of structure the accounting system will be the responsibility of the Finance Director and is centralised and strictly controlled. Study the diagram below.

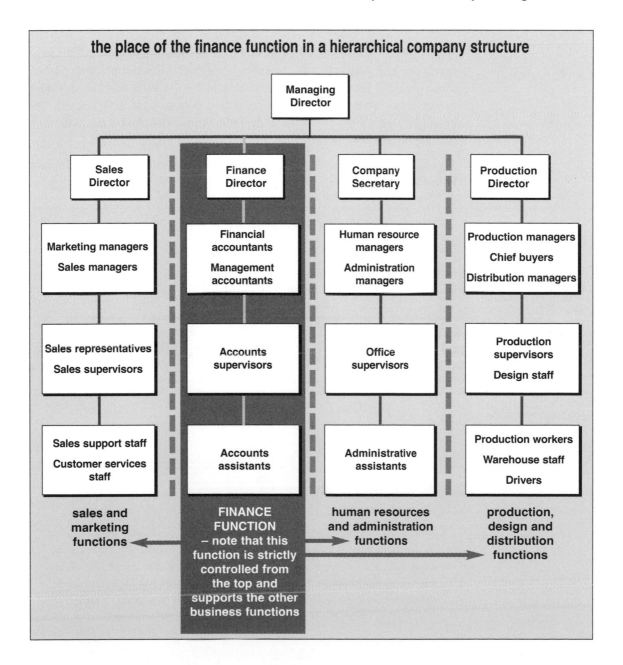

the place of the finance function in a hierarchical company structure

Managing Director

Sales Director | Finance Director | Company Secretary | Production Director

Marketing managers / Sales managers | Financial accountants / Management accountants | Human resource managers / Administration managers | Production managers / Chief buyers / Distribution managers

Sales representatives / Sales supervisors | Accounts supervisors | Office supervisors | Production supervisors / Design staff

Sales support staff / Customer services staff | Accounts assistants | Administrative assistants | Production workers / Warehouse staff / Drivers

sales and marketing functions | FINANCE FUNCTION – note that this function is strictly controlled from the top and supports the other business functions | human resources and administration functions | production, design and distribution functions

organisational structure – small business

It is appreciated that this chapter has so far concentrated on large organisations. It is more than likely that the workplace you decide to study, or the scenario provided in an AAT Case Study, will be **smaller businesses** or **voluntary organisations**. The large majority of businesses in the UK are, in fact, small businesses with fifty or fewer employees.

The organisational structure of a small business is therefore more likely to be 'flat' with the boss at the top and a variety of 'functions' or small departments under his or her direct control.

One of these functions will, of course, be the **accounting function**. This may involve a line manager who oversees a number of assistants and reports directly to the business owner. It may also be the case that the business owner looks after some of the accounting functions himself/herself, for example negotiating discounts and credit terms with major customers or completing the VAT Return.

This type of business is illustrated in the 'flat structure business' diagram below.

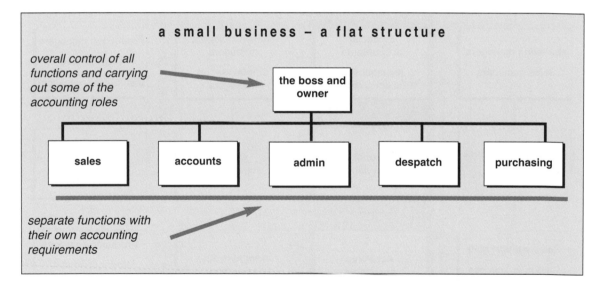

Report writing hint

When you describe the accounting system of your chosen organisation in the beginning of your Report you will need to identify the type of organisational structure used as it may help to explain problems within the accounting system. For example, a flat structure may lead to lack of co-ordination between different functions, and a hierarchical structure may lead to poor communication between the different levels.

FUNCTIONS OF AN ACCOUNTING SYSTEM

Your studies require you to look critically at the existing accounting system and to identify areas for improvement in both the system itself and the way in which it is managed.

A typical accounting system carries out a number of functions, shown in the diagram below. It is the responsibility of the management to ensure that it operates smoothly.

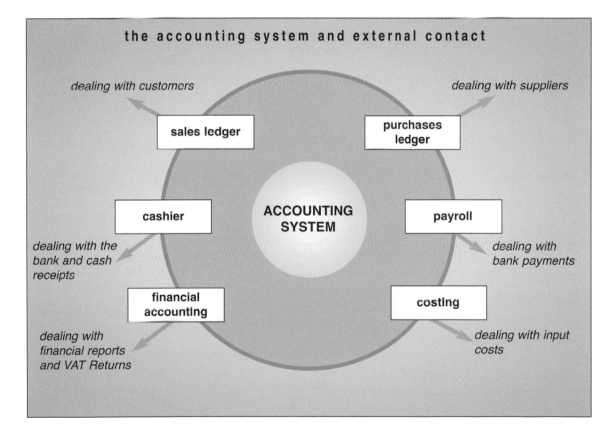

It is important that the accounting system is not seen to operate in isolation. Part of your assessment requirement is to analyse the way in which the accounting system integrates with the other internal functions of the organisation.

If the organisation is a manufacturing business, these other functions might include production, human resources, sales and marketing, administration.

Study the diagram on the next page to see how the accounting system inter-relates with some of the other internal functions of the organisation.

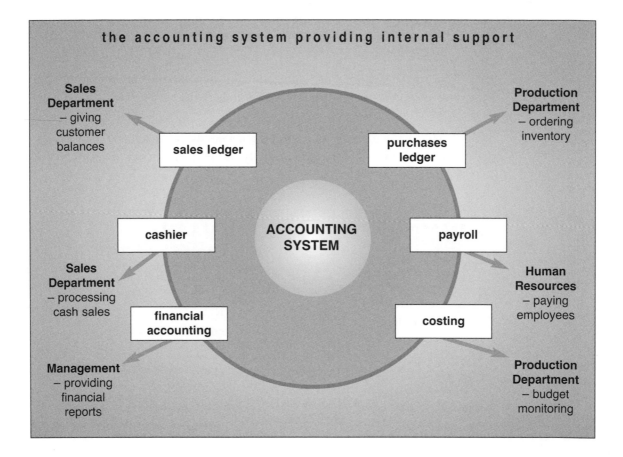

the accounting system providing internal support

Sales Department
– giving customer balances

sales ledger

purchases ledger

Production Department
– ordering inventory

cashier

ACCOUNTING SYSTEM

payroll

Sales Department
– processing cash sales

Human Resources
– paying employees

financial accounting

costing

Management
– providing financial reports

Production Department
– budget monitoring

Report writing hint

When you write about the accounting system of your chosen organisation you will need to analyse the way in which the organisation structures its accounting system. Some form of structure chart would be a useful aid, and could be included within the Appendices.

The analysis might identify weaknesses in the way the system is structured, in the way it is managed and in the way in which it communicates with people – eg customers or suppliers – **outside** the organisation.

The analysis should also look at the way in which the accounting system deals with other functions **inside** the organisation. A good starting point is to look at communications between the various departments. Is the system at fault at all?

THE NEED FOR GOOD COMMUNICATION

lines of communication in an accounting system

When studying the workplace you have chosen or the scenario in the AAT Case Study you will need to analyse the effectiveness of the communication between people in the accounting function itself – in addition to the communication between people in other functions, eg sales.

The diagram below illustrates the lines of communication between accounting employees in a large company. The accounting system here is subdivided into the areas of financial and management accounting.

The boxes with the dark grey background all represent specific accounting roles. You will see that the structure is set out in a series of layers of authority and responsibility.

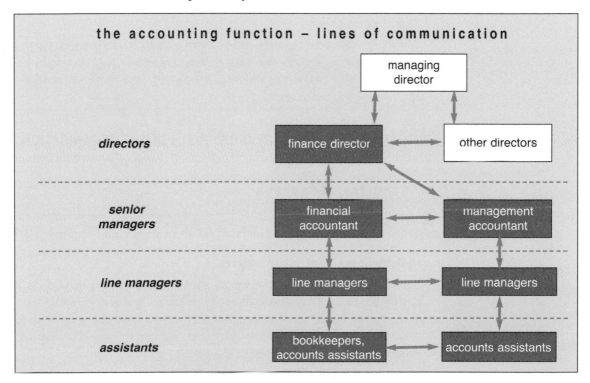

management information systems

A large organisation is often served by a **Management Information System (MIS).** This is a computer-based system which provides up-to-date, accurate and relevant information to management. An efficient MIS will enable management to make informed decisions promptly.

By 'management' we mean all levels of management, from line managers (supervisors) through to the Finance Director. Clearly the type and level of information required will vary according to the role of the manager and the type of decision expected of that manager. Examples of the type of data produced by an accounting MIS include:

- sales figures for products and regions
- inventory levels
- customer account details, ranging from balances to detailed reports such as the Aged Trade Receivables Analysis
- budget reports showing variances
- profitability reports by product

You will see from this range of information that decision-making can range from 'Do we allow this customer any more credit?' through to 'Do we continue to manufacture this product?'

Report writing hint

When you write about the accounting system of your chosen organisation you will need to assess the MIS, if it is available. Does it enable management to make the required decisions? Is it communicated effectively within the accounting system? Can it be improved?

CONTROL OF RESOURCES BY INDIVIDUALS IN THE ORGANISATION

the need for resources

Adequate **resources** are essential to the functioning of an organisation. All come at a cost. Resources can be classified under four main headings:

- **equipment and material resources**

  These include premises in which to work and equipment needed on a day-to-day basis. They also include the materials that may be used – raw materials, inventory and consumables such as biros and photocopy paper. A car manufacturer will clearly have a greater need for equipment and material resources in a factory than a firm of insurance brokers working from a town centre office. The important point here is that in both cases the resources will need to be adequate.

- **human resources**

  This term is now used widely to describe the 'people' function in organisations. There is always a need for the right number of appropriately skilled people to work within an organisation, whether in a management or an operational role.

■ **information**

This is an essential resource and must be readily available to whoever needs it within the organisation. Computer-based systems with up-to-date and accurate information are the ideal solution (see last section). Information in a manufacturing or retail business, for example, will include product specifications, prices, inventory levels, customer orders, supplier orders. A travel agency will need different types of information, but equally, the data will need to be accurate and up-to-date and on computer screen.

■ **financial resources**

This term means 'money' which is either available currently or can be made available within a set time period to allow spending in line with a particular budget allocation. This is probably the most critical type of resource for the functioning of the organisation. It affects all areas.

control of resources by individuals

As part of your investigation you should examine the way in which individuals within the organisation control the supply of the various resources described above. Control of resources is normally dictated by the various levels of budget within an organisation.

For example, the production or staffing budget of a business is likely to be decided upon at director level and the departmental budget will be the responsibility of the departmental manager. Line managers (supervisors) will also have decisions to make about control of resources – for example they may be given the power to allow staff to work overtime and to order small items of office equipment. Employees at assistant level will also have control of resources at a reduced level, for example ordering stationery items or tea and coffee for the rest room. It is all a question of level and scale.

The diagram below sets out the hierarchy of individuals who will make decisions about controlling resources; it shows 'level and scale'.

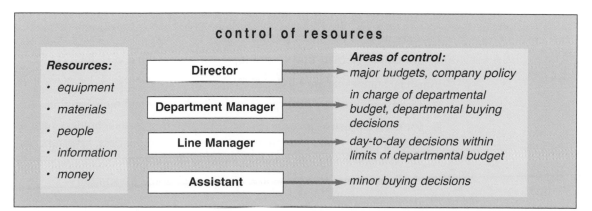

errors and fraud within the system

The control of resources brings with it the opportunity both for error and for fraud. Both can be avoided with the enforcement of checking and monitoring procedures. **Error** includes situations involving over-ordering of materials – for example ordering 5,000 suspension files instead of 100 where the units ordered were boxes of 50 rather than individual files. **Fraud** is a fact of life where control of resources is concerned. It can range from a director siphoning off funds by 'fiddling the books' to the supposedly innocent pilfering of biros and stationery at assistant level. The issue of fraud is covered in detail in the next chapter.

Report writing hint

When you write about the accounting system of your chosen organisation you will need to identify the individuals who control resources, and comment on the scope of the decisions they can make and the control mechanisms that exist.

You should look for areas in which efficiency in the control of resources and information provision could be improved.

THE USE OF FINANCIAL STATEMENTS

As you will know from your studies, organisations produce financial statements on a regular basis. The number and extent of the financial statements will depend on the type and size of the organisation. Preparation of the data for these statements is all part of the regular accounting work carried out by an organisation, although normally the final statements will be produced by the organisation's accountants.

The main statements produced are:

- **statement of profit or loss**
- **statement of financial position**
- **statement of cash flows** – not to be confused with a cash budget

Financial statements are produced:

- for **internal use** by the organisation for planning and budgeting reasons
- for **external use** to provide financial information to stakeholders such as shareholders, banks, suppliers, pressure groups, possible investors and Government bodies such as HM Revenue & Customs

We will now summarise these uses and provide some illustrations.

financial statements for internal use

Financial statements – and the **ratios** that can be extracted from them – provide management with information about the financial state of the organisation. They will enable the management to analyse past performance and also, in the **master budget**, project future performance.

Areas of particular interest to senior management include:

statement of profit or loss
- sales performance
- gross and net profit margins
- comparison of areas of expense

statement of financial position
- liquidity
- gearing
- return on capital employed

statement of cash flows
- explanation of changes in the cash position of a company
- investments made in assets
- sources of financing

financial statements for external use

Financial statements – and the **ratios** that can be extracted from them – are also very important sources of information for external stakeholders who need to assess the financial position of the organisation. For example:

■ **Banks**

When lending, banks need to assess the financial performance and financial strength of an organisation. They need to make sure that any lending can be repaid and also that there are sufficient assets available for security. They will want to see, in the case of a limited company:

- a statement of profit or loss to check that profit is being generated
- a statement of financial position to ensure that a company is not over-geared (ie there is not too much borrowing already in relation to equity)
- a cash budget to confirm that the company will have adequate cash flow over the next twelve months (note that a 'cash budget' is not the same as a 'statement of cash flows')

■ **Suppliers**

The credit control function of many suppliers requires sight of the accounts of prospective customers – either directly or through credit reference agencies – so that they can carry out ratio analysis before granting credit terms.

■ **HM Revenue & Customs**

The statement of profit or loss will provide the source of the data for the calculation of tax due on profits made.

■ **Shareholders and investors**

The published financial statements of public limited companies contain the statement of profit or loss, statement of financial position and the statement of cash flows. These and the investment ratios they provide enable owners of shares and prospective investors to assess the return they are likely to make on the company shares.

Extracts from the financial statements of a quoted public limited company are shown below. The money amounts are quoted in £ millions.

statement of profit or loss

Operating profit		**3,457**	3,169
Share of post-tax profits of joint ventures and associates	13	**33**	110
Finance income	5	**265**	116
Finance costs	5	**(579)**	(478)
Profit before tax	3	**3,176**	2,917
Taxation	6	**(840)**	(779)
Profit for the year		**2,336**	2,138
Attributable to:			
Owners of the parent		**2,327**	2,133
Minority interests		**9**	5
		2,336	2,138
Earnings per share			
Basic	9	**29.33p**	27.14p
Diluted	9	**29.19p**	26.96p

statement of financial position

Financial liabilities			
Borrowings	21	**(11,744)**	(12,391)	(5,972)
Derivative financial instruments and other liabilities	22	**(776)**	(302)	(322)
Post-employment benefit obligations	28	**(1,840)**	(1,494)	(838)
Deferred tax liabilities	6	**(795)**	(676)	(791)
Provisions	26	**(172)**	(200)	(23)
		(15,327)	(15,063)	(7,946)
Net assets		**14,681**	12,906	11,873
Equity			
Share capital	29	**399**	395	393
Share premium account		**4,801**	4,638	4,511
Other reserves		**40**	40	40
Retained earnings		**9,356**	7,776	6,842

statement of cash flows

Cash flows from operating activities			
Cash generated from operations	31	**5,947**	4,978
Interest paid		**(690)**	(562)
Corporation tax paid		**(512)**	(456)
Net cash from operating activities		**4,745**	3,960
Cash flows from investing activities			
Acquisition of subsidiaries, net of cash acquired		**(65)**	(1,275)
Proceeds from sale of property, plant and equipment		**1,820**	994
Purchase of property, plant and equipment and investment property		**(2,855)**	(4,487)

> **Report writing hint**
>
> You are not required to examine the financial statements of the organisation in your Report but you will need to explain how they are used by the organisation and its stakeholders.

CHANGES BROUGHT ABOUT BY EXTERNAL REGULATION

Very often the smooth running of an accounts system can be disturbed by forces outside the control of the organisation. Changes may be required because of the introduction of new external regulations or changes to existing rules.

Whatever the case, the accounting system should be ready to react to any external changes and have the **internal policies and procedures** established and in hand in order to be able to deal with them. Examples include:

- **a change in accounting terminology**

  You will know from your studies that there is move away from UK accounting terminology to international terminology which has been established by the International Accounting Standards Board (IASB) through its IASs and IFRSs. These are currently applicable to larger limited companies in the UK. It is likely that this terminology will eventually supersede the existing UK terminology, meaning that more and more organisations over time will need to refer to 'trade receivables' rather than 'debtors' and to 'inventory' rather than to 'stock.'

  Organisations will need to amend much documentation and invest in staff training to cope with these changes. Again, internal policies and procedures will need to be established to deal with this.

- **a change in Company Law**

  Company law in the UK changed with the passing of the Companies Act 2006. This affected the way in which limited companies operated and included provisions which affected their accounting systems. For example, the requirement for authorised share capital was abolished – this affected the Statement of Financial Position.

  Companies and their advisors will therefore need to be alert to this type of change in legislation.

■ **a change in the VAT rate**

This can seriously disturb the smooth running of any VAT-registered business. It particularly affects retail businesses, involving the repricing of goods on the shelf and in the warehouse, reprinting of catalogues, amendments on the website, amendments to invoicing software and the training of staff to deal with a confused public.

Most large retailers will have internal policies and procedures in hand to deal with this situation.

Set out below is an email illustrating the way in which the accounting system is affected by a change in VAT rate and the way in which it will have to communicate with other functions in the company to advise the implications of the change.

EMAIL

To: All Departmental Managers

From   Alex Rowlands, Finance Director

Subject: Increase in standard rate VAT from 20% to 22.5% w.e.f. 4 January

---

As you will know, standard rate VAT is due to increase from 20% to 22.5% on 4 January.

It is essential that you all carry out the necessary procedures to ensure that the changeover goes smoothly and that our customers are aware of the price changes. I would like to highlight a number of key areas to you:

1 Accounts Department: Sales and Purchases Ledger should ensure that the Sage settings for VAT on invoices and credit notes are amended to 22.5%.

2 Accounts Department: Management Accounting Section should ensure that the Excel spreadsheets for cash budgets are amended to show the increase in output VAT received.

3 Marketing and Sales: all publicity literature quoting VAT inclusive prices should be withdrawn before 4 January and revised prices calculated and quoted on new publicity material. The website should be similarly checked for prices and the VAT rate on the online shop amended accordingly from 4 January.

4 Warehouse and shop: any price stickers or barcodes on stock showing pre-increase prices should be removed and replaced by new price stickers and barcodes.

Please ensure that in each case detailed instructions are issued to your staff. These instructions are available as standing instructions in the Company Procedures Manual.

Regards

Alex Rowlands

inspiration page – for your notes

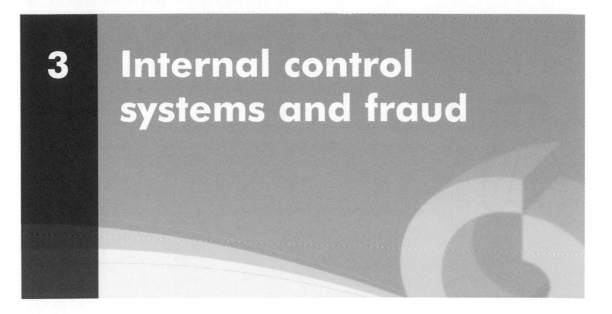

3 Internal control systems and fraud

this chapter covers...

This chapter starts where the last chapter finished, by dealing with the external regulations that affect accounting practice. Some of these are required by legislation and affect areas such as taxation, auditing and the regulation of limited companies.

Others are 'accounting standards' set both in the UK and internationally by independent accounting standards bodies.

The main part of this chapter explains the internal control systems that are set up in an organisation to implement all the requirements of external regulations and other organisational requirements.

The chapter describes in detail:

■ the different types of fraud that can be committed within an organisation

■ the risk of fraud occurring within an organisation

■ the areas vulnerable to fraud

■ the need to design a system so that fraud is minimised, can be easily detected and dealt with as appropriate

EXTERNAL REGULATIONS AFFECTING ACCOUNTING PRACTICE

legislation

The term 'legislation' covers a wide range of regulations based on UK Acts of Parliament and European Directives. Organisations are affected by a number of legal regulations affecting the way in which an accounting system operates. Examples include:

- **taxation regulations** – affecting areas such as:
  - PAYE for individuals on the payroll: income tax, National Insurance and other deductions
  - Value Added Tax: VAT returns, invoice format, rates applied
  - corporation tax paid by limited companies

- **company law** – set out in the Companies Acts – requires that company financial statements (of larger companies) should be audited; these statements are to be drawn up in a set format and sent to shareholders; larger companies also have to send full versions of these statements to Companies House where they can be accessed by the public

- **data protection law** – set out in the Data Protection Act 1998 – protects data (including financial data) relating to individual customers

- **late payment law** – set out in the Late Payment of Commercial Debts Regulations 2013 – allows suppliers to charge interest on late payment of invoices

UK and international accounting standards

The **Financial Reporting Council** (FRC) is a unified, independent regulator which:

- sets, monitors and enforces accounting and auditing standards
- oversees the regulatory activities of the professional accountancy bodies
- regulates audit
- promotes high standards of internal regulation within companies ('corporate governance')

The membership of the Council includes wide and balanced representation at the highest levels from the business, investor, professional and other communities interested in corporate reporting and governance.

The FRC promotes good financial reporting through its Committees and Councils, which include the **Accounting Council** and the **Audit and Assurance Council**.

The FRC takes an active role in relation to the internal regulation of companies, ensuring that they comply with company law, accounting standards, and auditing standards.

Accounting standards have been developed over many years and are now the responsibility of the **Accounting Council**, a part of the FRC, to provide the rules, or framework, of accounting. The intention has been to reduce the variety of alternative accounting treatments. This framework for accounting is represented in the UK by **Statements of Standard Accounting Practice** (SSAPs) and **Financial Reporting Standards** (FRSs).

As you will know from your other studies, many companies – European (including UK plcs) and worldwide – now prepare their financial statements in accordance with **International Financial Reporting Standards** (IFRSs). It is anticipated that international financial reporting standards will eventually replace the UK Standards.

International Standards on Auditing (ISAs) are also gradually being introduced; these will set down guidelines for the way in which UK businesses are audited.

Report writing hint

When you write about the proposed change to the accounting system of your chosen organisation you will need to provide evidence that it takes account of any change in external factors such as changes in the law (eg company regulation, tax rates) and changes in accounting standards.

THE NEED FOR POLICIES AND PROCEDURES

External regulations – such as legislation – are only of any use if an organisation regulates its employees and keeps them up-to-date by issuing formal internal sets of rules and guidelines. These are often referred to as **Policies and Procedures**.

what do Policies and Procedures cover?

Illustrated on the opposite page is an internal document issued by a large company outlining the introduction of new Policies and Procedures for the retention and disposal of records throughout the business.

'Records' can be paper-based or electronic. In this case, the document produced by each function in the business – sales, administration, accounting and finance – will set out:

- what records should be retained and at what level of security – ie if they should be locked up or not
- the period of time for which the records should be stored
- what records should be disposed of (ie shredded or wiped from a computer storage medium)

In the case of the **Accounting and Finance** function, this could include:

- retention of financial documents such as invoices, bank statements, payroll records – often for six years
- safe disposal of these records after this period
- immediate safe disposal of confidential details such as credit card details from customers sent in with mailed orders

In this document the need for new Policies and Procedures is made clear:

"The company is obliged under information legislation to have retention/disposal schedules for all its corporate records. Without clear retention/disposal policies the company risks falling foul of the Data Protection Act, Freedom of Information Act, and Public Record Act."

RECORD RETENTION AND DISPOSAL – NEW POLICIES AND PROCEDURES

Our Policies and Procedures are the main reference material for people in each Department.

All formal procedures and work systems are outlined in these documents which give managers and staff the rules and guidelines.

The company is obliged under information legislation to have retention/disposal schedules for all its corporate records. Without clear retention/disposal policies the company risks falling foul of the Data Protection Act, Freedom of Information Act, and Public Record Act. Failure to dispose of records in a timely and efficient manner can lead to criticism from the Information Commissioner and Adjudicator.

Currently, information relating to how long we should be keeping records is scattered throughout operational guidance. Quite often this retention/disposal information is out-of-date and/or the reasons behind why particular time periods were chosen have been forgotten.

The people making decisions regarding retention/disposal timescales need to understand the different reasons that may effect their decision.

These new Policies and Procedures:

- lay down the company policy for documenting retention information
- explain why a retention policy is needed
- identify numerous reasons that can effect the retention period decision, and contain a good practice guide on how to construct a retention schedule

INTERNAL CONTROL IN AN ACCOUNTING SYSTEM

Any accounting system will have certain elements in common, whether it is a company Accounts Department, a Local Authority Purchasing Department or a charitable organisation's fundraising section. It will:

■ deal with money – handling cash

■ need to make payments and issue cheques

■ have 'levels of authority' within the system

■ need to make decisions over ordering and purchasing

■ need to set budgets for spending

■ need to organise its accounting records

Unless the management is happy to let everything become totally disorganised, the accounting system will need to establish various **rules and regulations** which will establish an **internal control system,** for example:

■ the establishing of **money limits** for certain transactions

■ the definition of **levels of responsibility** for **authorising** transactions

■ the need for **referral of decision making** to another person when required

Illustrated on the opposite page are extracts from a **Policies and Procedures** internal control document issued by the Accounts and Finance Department of a medium-sized business. Read through this and you will see that there are a number of examples of the three areas of internal control outlined above. These have been extracted and are shown below.

---

money limits

All orders of £1,000 or more must be authorised by the budget holder.

All cheques for £1,000 or over require two signatories.

Petty cash will be topped up on the 'imprest' system, where the amount spent is reimbursed. It is intended for small items, up to £20.

authorisation

All invoices must be authorised for payment by the budget holder.

Salary payments require the signature of the Accounts Manager or Financial Controller, plus one other.

referral to another person or higher authority

Budget holders will discuss with the Financial Controller appropriate parameters, plus maximum allowed deviations before the budget holder or senior manager is brought in; this will be documented.

Finance must be informed if there are queries delaying authorisation (of payments) or if payment is to be withheld for any reason.

POLICIES AND PROCEDURES STATEMENT– ACCOUNTING AND FINANCE (extracts)

Books of account and records

Proper accounting records will be kept. The accounts systems is based around computer facilities, using Sage and Excel, but manual/paper records will also be used if appropriate. The following records will be kept:

- Appropriate control accounts (bank control, petty cash control, VAT control, salary control)
- Monthly trial balances
- Petty cash and bank accounts will be reconciled at least monthly
- VAT Returns produced on the required quarterly cycle

Ordering supplies and services

Budget holders can place orders for goods or services within their budget areas, subject only to cash-flow restraints. All orders of £1,000 or more must be authorised by the budget holder, except for specific areas of expenditure where written procedures have been agreed. Under £1,000, the budget holder may delegate all ordering as appropriate. Budget holders will discuss with the Financial Controller appropriate parameters, plus maximum allowed deviations before the budget holder or senior manager is brought in, which will be documented.

Payment authorisation and Purchases Ledger

All invoices must be authorised for payment by the budget holder, although the actual checking of details may be delegated. The authorising department is responsible for checking invoices for accuracy in terms of figures and conformity with the order placed, that the services or goods have been received, and following up any problems. Finance must be informed if there are queries delaying authorisation or if payment is to be withheld for any reason.

A Purchases Ledger is operated by Finance. All incoming invoices are to be passed to Finance section as soon as they arrive. Invoices will be recorded in the Purchases Ledger within two days, unless there are coding problems. They are then passed on to budget holders for authorisation. Once authorised as above, suppliers will be paid within the appropriate timescale.

Cheque writing and signing

Signatories will only be drawn from senior staff and directors, and any new signatory must be approved by the directors before the bank is notified. All cheques for £1,000 or over require two signatories. Cheque signatories should check that the expenditure has been authorised by the appropriate person before signing the cheque. Salary payments require the signature of the Accounts Manager or Financial Controller, plus one other. Cheques should be filled in completely (with payee, amount in words and figures, and date) before cheques are signed.

Handling of cash

Petty cash will be topped up on the 'imprest' system, where the amount spent is reimbursed. It is intended for small items, up to £20. Anything over this should be paid by cheque where possible. The imprest has a balance limit of £250. The petty cash balance will be reconciled when restoring the imprest balance, or monthly if this is more frequent. All cash collected from Finance will be signed for, and receipts will be issued for all cash returned.

> **Report writing hint**
>
> When you are investigating an accounting system in the workplace, try to obtain access to the relevant Policies and Procedures document. It may not be called precisely this, but may be set out as an operations manual or even separate sets of instructions for each section of the system, eg purchasing, petty cash or sales invoicing.

reviewing the accounting system

Your review of an accounting system, whether it is in the workplace or set out in an AAT Case Study will be covered in full in Chapter 5.

You will need to appreciate that if an accounting system has weaknesses it will be because the internal control system – as seen on the previous two pages – will be deficient in one way or another. This will lead to various possible problems:

- **errors being made** because people do not know the correct way of doing things
- errors being made **and not being picked up** because the processes are not being checked properly

and lastly . . .

- **fraud being committed** because the internal control system is deficient and the opportunity for fraud is there for the taking

TYPES OF FRAUD

Fraud is an unfortunate fact of life within organisations. It sometimes hits the headlines, as when a merchant banker's PA diverted over £1 million of her employer's funds into designer clothes, cars, speedboats, and general high living. This is obviously an extreme example which makes good material for the media, but the principle involved is the same as the employee who walks off with the employer's stationery or petty cash, or who sneaks out of work an hour early to watch a football match.

Fraud within an organisation can therefore be described as an activity which presents a threat of some form of loss to the employer:

- **loss of money**, eg theft of petty cash
- **loss of inventory**, eg theft of products by supermarket staff
- **loss of time**, eg disappearing from work to do something else during contracted work hours

It is the responsibility of the management of an organisation to:

- identify areas where the **risk of fraud** exists and to grade the seriousness of the risk in each case

- set up **control system**s involving all staff to alert management to possible occurrence of fraud

- **monitor** those control systems on a regular basis to ensure that they are working

- **deal with** any incidence of fraud in an appropriate way, whether it be a formal warning or calling in the police

These will be dealt with in the course of this chapter. First, however, it is important to define in more detail what we mean by 'fraud'.

some definitions

Fraud covers a variety of offences, but a general definition of fraud is:

the use of deception with the intention of obtaining an advantage, avoiding an obligation or causing loss to someone else or to an organisation

Fraud is a criminal activity and is covered in the UK by a number of laws:

theft	dishonestly taking someone else's property (Theft Act)
false accounting	dishonestly destroying, defacing, concealing or falsifying an accounting record for personal gain or to cause loss to someone else (Theft Act)
bribery and corruption	taking or giving a bribe that might influence the actions of others (Prevention of Corrupt Practices Acts)
deception	obtaining property, money, services or evading liability by deception (Theft Act)

practical examples of fraud

In practical terms fraud is normally a combination of any of the following:

- **theft** of property or money or information (eg someone copying and selling the company's customer database to a competitor)

- **falsification** of records so that property or money is passed to the wrong person (eg someone 'fiddling' the payroll)

- **collusion** – ie a 'set-up' between an employee and someone else outside the organisation, eg false invoices sent in by an outsider for supplies that were never made and authorised and paid by the person 'on the inside'

public examples of fraud

There are many examples of fraud which are made public. Students involved in the public sector would find it useful to investigate the HM Treasury Fraud Reports, available as downloads from the website www.hm-treasury.gov.uk. These contain examples of fraud in local authorities and Government departments. Types of fraud in the private sector are very similar. The examples below have been adapted from cases reported by a leading insurance company.

REPORTED CASES OF FRAUD

Theft of fuel stocks – *Total Loss £25,000*

A local authority had their own fuel pumps for supplying their motor vehicles. The employee in charge stole fuel over a long period as the inventory checks were inadequate.

Payroll fraud: fictitious employees – *Total Loss £10,000*

The manager of an industrial cleaning company invented bogus employees, put them on the payroll and then cashed their pay cheques.

Bank deposits: teeming and lading – *In 10 months a total of £7,000 was stolen.*

A clerk in charge of a sub post office stole cash receipts due to be paid into the local bank. This was covered up by delaying paying in at the bank and altering the paying-in slips relating to subsequent deposits. Stealing money received from one source and then using money received from other sources to cover it up is known as 'teeming and lading'.

Cheque printing machine – *Total Loss £25,000*

A ledger clerk responsible for making regular payment of rent for advertising was in charge of a machine that printed cheques. Numerous small cheques were made out by him for the correct amounts but payable to him. It was several months before complaints from creditors, (who had not received their cheques) were investigated and the fraud uncovered.

Collusion: stock control system – *Total Loss £1 million*

A well known national company was defrauded by two gangs of employees working at the same location. The losses involved collusion between warehousemen and drivers who used the spare capacity on vehicles to remove goods from the depot. False information was entered into the computerised inventory control system and their activities were only discovered when the police reported finding large amounts of the particular product in the hands of third parties.

Collusion: fictitious sub-contractors – *Total Loss exceeded £500,000*

A major contractor with well established control systems to approve payments were the victims of fraud by a section supervisor in collusion with a computer operator. Cheques were made out to fictitious sub-contractors and despatched to private addresses.

> **Report writing hint**
>
> When you write about your analysis of the current accounting system of your chosen organisation you will need to provide evidence that you have investigated potential areas of fraud. You will need to be aware of the various types of fraud that can be committed.

RISK ASSESSMENT AND FRAUD

risk assessment – the role of management

Assessment of **fraud risk** is part of the **risk assessment** process which is the responsibility of organisations in both the private and the public sectors.

In the case of limited companies (private sector), the Turnbull Report has stated that directors have responsibility for ensuring that risk management practices are established as part of an effective internal control system.

In the public sector the guiding document to fraud risk is HM Treasury's 'Managing the Risk of Fraud – a Guide for Managers' available as a download from www.hm-treasury.gov.uk

The assessment of risk generally by management follows a number of distinct stages. This process applies equally to the assessment of fraud risk:

- setting up a risk management group and identifying objectives
- identifying the areas of risk of fraud
- grading the scale of the risk in each case
- developing a strategy to manage that risk
- setting up systems to detect and deal with fraud, allocating responsibility
- getting the systems up and running
- monitoring the running of the system

the internal control system

A robust internal control system is essential if management is going to be able to detect and deal with fraud.

There are various techniques that can be used for making an internal control system 'fraud resistant':

■ **fraud staff**

Some very large organisations may appoint employees – eg ex-bank or ex-police staff – to work full-time on fraud prevention and detection.

■ **management responsibility**

Managers should be given specific areas of responsibility and answerability – eg sections of the Accounts Department – to ensure that fraud is kept to a minimum.

■ **management supervision**

Management – particularly line management – should supervise accounting activities on a regular basis. This involves overseeing and checking activities such as data entry to computers, making payments and payroll processing.

■ **segregation of duties**

The system should be set up so that duties which, when combined, could lead to fraud, are given to different people – ie they are segregated. For example, the cashier taking in cash for a business should ideally not be the same person who makes out the paying-in slip for the bank. The danger is that some of the cash may disappear into the cashier's pocket.

■ **lock & key**

Physical security – locking valuable items away – is a sure deterrent to theft. This does not only apply to cash: the tendency of items such as laptop computers and mobile phones to disappear has become a well-known and ever-increasing statistic.

■ **authorisation**

Some accounting activities may require authorisation by a nominated official. This ranges from the authorisation of petty cash, signing of cheques over a certain amount to the investing of liquid funds, eg placing £250,000 on a money market account. Clearly the larger the amount, the more senior the person giving authorisation.

detecting fraud

We have already seen the various areas in which fraud can occur. Fraud can be detected by the experienced manager by simple observation and through experience. Some of the tell-tale and danger signs include:

■ employees acting suspiciously – looking shifty and hiding paperwork

■ employees with higher levels of spending than you would expect from their income – the payroll clerk who has a new Porsche

- employees working long hours and taking less than the normal holiday entitlement – it is often when employees are away that other employees notice suspicious signs and uncover criminal activity
- employees who have a grudge against the organisation – they may have been passed over for promotion or they may even have a political or ethical axe to grind
- employees who are known to be short of money – they may be struggling with a high mortgage or may even have a drugs problem

grading likelihood and impact

Part of the process of the management of fraud risk is the decision about whether a risk is a **likely** one or not. The likelihood of risk can be divided into three levels:

- **high** – the likelihood of fraud is at a high level (disappearing biros)
- **moderate** – the likelihood is possible (theft of cash, collusion)
- **low** – the likelihood is remote (removal of assets from a company pension fund)

The risk of fraud occurring can also be given a **numerical value**: for example a range of 1 to 5, where the higher the risk the higher the number.

Risk assessment also needs to decide whether the **impact** of the fraud is significant. Impact can relate to the **financial state** of the organisation. A major loss through fraud could seriously affect profit and liquidity. For example, the fraudulent trading by an employee of Barings Bank led to its collapse. The fraud can also seriously affect employees, as in the Robert Maxwell case in which employees' pensions were appropriated by the Chairman and Chief Executive.

Generally speaking, frauds that are likely (the disappearing biro) have a lower impact than the remote risk (removal of assets from a company pension fund). The **impact** of a fraud can therefore be similarly graded:

- **high** – the effects of fraud are very serious for the organisation, affecting its profit and/or liquidity
- **moderate** – the effects of the fraud are significant but can be dealt with internally, or in some cases by the police (theft, collusion)
- **low** – the impact of the fraud is insignificant (petty pilfering)

using a matrix to grade fraud risk

Organisations sometimes use a matrix to assess the extent of fraud risk in an accounting system. The areas of the system in which the fraud might occur must first be identified, for example:

- cash payments
- cash receipts
- sales ledger
- purchases ledger
- expenses
- inventory control
- payroll
- fixed asset purchase

A matrix (or a section of a matrix) will then be drawn up for each of the areas identified. An example of entries in a typical matrix is illustrated below. The matrix might display:

- the identified risk area of the organisation
- the details of the type of fraud
- the role of the employee who may become involved in it
- any third party who may become involved through collusion
- the likelihood of the fraud (high, moderate, low)
- the impact of the fraud (high, moderate, low)

This matrix will then become a valuable tool which will enable management to assess the risks and establish an appropriate strategy for minimising them. Note that the format of the matrices you will encounter in your studies may vary. The example below is fairly typical and could be used in your Report.

accounting system fraud matrix – some sample entries

Details of Risk	Employees	Collusion	Likelihood	Impact
Payroll section: Stationery pilferage	payroll staff	none	high	low
Theft of cash	payroll staff	none	moderate	moderate
Payments to fictitious employees	payroll staff	third party recipients	moderate	moderate
Purchase ledger: Paying fictitious suppliers	buyer	third party recipients	moderate	moderate
etc . . . etc . . .				

> **Report writing hint**
>
> It is recommended that you should not only research into potential areas of fraud, but you should also identify each type of fraud and grade its **risk** (using a high/medium/low or a numerical system) and its **impact**, using some form of matrix – such as the one on the previous page.
>
> Remember, however, that you will need to be diplomatic with the organisation that you are dealing with, as fraud is a very sensitive issue.

FRAUD POLICY

Fraud detection is an important function in any internal control system. We have already seen earlier in this chapter some of the warning signs of fraud which managers should look out for as a matter of course. It is useful, however, for an organisation to set up a **Fraud Policy** which might include:

- a clear indication of which managers are responsible for which potential areas of fraud and at what levels

- setting up of control systems to help avoid fraud, eg strict checking, segregation of tasks and division of responsibilities, eg in the purchasing process the person who sets up a purchase order should not be the same as the person who approves it or the person who writes out cheques should not be the same person who signs it (unless maybe it is for a very small amount)

- the regular monitoring of the control systems to ensure that they are working satisfactorily and are amended from time-to-time as circumstances require

- decisions about which type of frauds are significant (eg moderate and high risk) and should be acted upon and those which should be generally guarded against but which are low risk and do not require strict disciplinary action (eg the 'borrowed' biro)

- the need for an anti-fraud 'culture', ie instilling in employees the notion that any form of fraud (including the 'borrowed' biro) is inherently wrong and alerting them to the risks that exist

- following on from the last point, the mechanism should exist for 'whistle-blowing', ie for employees to alert the management if they become aware of any fraudulent goings-on at any level of the organisation; the employee in this case is given protection by the Public Interest Disclosure Act 1998

action taken to deal with fraud

As part of its Fraud Policy, an organisation should set up a system which ensures that the correct action is taken when:

- fraud is discovered by someone within the organisation
- fraud is reported by someone outside the organisation – the police, for example

Areas which should be dealt with are:

- provision of clear directions to managers about whom to contact when a fraud is discovered
- in a large organisation the appointment of a senior manager with special responsibility for fraud who can take responsibility for any major occurrences
- directions for disciplinary procedures for occurrences of fraud which will not have to involve the police and possible prosecution
- directions for how to deal with a case of fraud which will involve the notification of the police and may result in a criminal prosecution
- directions for how to deal with a case of fraud which is reported to the organisation by the police (eg the discovery of stolen inventory or a bank reporting suspicious money transactions) – and which may result in a criminal prosecution

As you will have gathered from this chapter, fraud is inevitable. The lesson for the organisation is – be prepared.

Report writing hint

Your Report should include a note of any formal Fraud Policy, and if this does not exist, details of managerial control systems and any arrangements made for these systems to be monitored. Evidence of the introduction of any anti-fraud culture could also be included.

---

some useful websites

www.sfo.gov.uk   www.icaew.com   www.hm-treasury.gov.uk

In order to access information about fraud you are likely to have to carry out a website search on 'fraud'.

This chapter concludes with two Case Studies on fraud and analysis of fraud published by HM Treasury. They should provide you with an understanding of how a weakness in the accounting system can make fraud possible.

Travel and subsistence fraud

Case description

This fraud involved an employee who travelled regularly on official business. He **set his own programme** of visits which was **not checked** by his line manager. He then regularly **submitted fraudulent travel and subsistence claims** which included examples of:

- Claiming subsistence allowances **in excess of entitlement;**

- Claiming for overnight stays in hotels when in fact he had **stayed with friends or family;**

- Claiming for **visits not made;**

- **Forging** authorising signatures;

- **Inflating claims** by altering details on claim forms **after authorisation** by countersigning officer.

These claims were paid by the finance team despite the **lack of receipts**, invoices or other supporting documents to verify his expenditure. Travel and subsistence **guidance was also out of date** and consequently had **fallen into disuse**.

The fraud came to light when his office tried to contact him at a hotel where he claimed to be staying. An investigation uncovered a large number of fraudulent claims spanning several years and the officer was eventually prosecuted.

Control weaknesses

- Inadequate guidance on submitting, authorising and paying claims;

- Inadequate supervision by line management;

- Failure of countersigning officer to verify that journeys had been made;

- Inadequate control exercised by countersigning officer in returning signed claim forms to the claimant rather than passing them directly to the finance team;

- Inadequate checks by finance teams to query amendments to claims, verify countersignatures and ensure that receipts and invoices were included to substantiate claims;

- Absence of spot checks on claims by the finance team management.

Cash handling fraud

Case description

Transactions involving receipts of cash or cheques are high risk. Of the cases of staff fraud reported to the Treasury each year, a significant proportion involves misappropriation of cash. In this sample case, a member of staff committed a number of frauds over a period of five years, resulting in a loss of over £10,000.

The organisation's business included the **receipt of cheques** through the post and cash and cheques over the counter. It was the responsibility of the member of staff to receive, record and **prepare the receipts for banking**. She had been in the job several years and her line managers, who trusted her implicitly, had given her **sole responsibility for these duties**. They were no longer carrying out checks or monitoring the process.

She would arrive early each morning, usually before her colleagues, **and open the post on her own**. Money handed in over the counters was also passed to her for banking. However, she **did not record or account for the cheques or money** prior to banking. She would, however, complete a daily cash balance record as part of the **banking reconciliation procedures**, but by this time she had already removed some of the cash and a number of cheques. There were **no independent cross-checks** between the documentation which came with the receipts and the amounts sent for banking. To make matters worse **written procedures were out of date** and had fallen into disuse.

The fraud came to light during the officer's **infrequent absences on leave**. A minor query by a member of the public regarding a previous payment led to an unexplained difference between the amount quoted in the documentation accompanying the payment and the amount recorded by the officer and banked.

Internal audit were brought in to carry out an initial investigation. They identified major discrepancies between records of receipts kept by counter staff, documentation accompanying payments from members of the public and the amounts being banked. The police were called in and under questioning the officer admitted the offences. She had opened a bank account with the initials of the organisation and had been paying in cash and cheques over a five year period. The case was taken to court and on conviction she was given a custodial sentence and had to repay the amounts stolen.

Control weaknesses

- Lack of separation of duties between post opening, preparation of cash and cheques for banking and reconciliation of amounts banked

- Inadequate supervision and monitoring by line management

- Absence of management checks of accounting records, cash balances or bank reconciliations

- Over-reliance on the honesty and integrity of one individual

- Lack of adequate written instructions

- Unawareness of implications of reluctance to use leave entitlement

- The internal audit report also identified organisational factors which had contributed to the fraud. The main ones were:

  ➢ The organisation had not assessed the risk of fraud;

  ➢ There was no policy statement on fraud;

  ➢ Line managers were not clear about their responsibilities;

  ➢ Manuals and procedures were poorly structured and out of date.

Professional ethics and sustainability

this chapter covers...

The last chapter described the importance of recognising the specific danger areas of possible fraud within an accounting system.

This chapter covers two issues which will have an impact on the way in which organisations are run and which will affect the accounting system: professional ethics and sustainability.

Your studies require you to carry out an evaluation of the way in which these two issues are dealt with in the accounting system of an organisation. The evaluation will consider:

■ **Professional ethics***, ie the principles on which professional behaviour at work are based:*

- *integrity*
- *objectivity*
- *professional competence and due care*
- *confidentiality*
- *professional behaviour*

■ **Sustainability***, ie the extent to which the organisation has adopted policies of 'sustainable development' which is based on three main factors: economic growth, environmental protection and social equality.*

These three factors can involve:

- *encouraging sales and profitability in a responsible way*
- *the implementation of 'green' policies such as recycling and energy saving*
- *adopting 'corporate social responsibility' (CSR), a policy formulated to encourage socially beneficial activities such as sponsoring sporting events*

PROFESSIONAL ETHICS

some revision

You will already have studied Professional Ethics before, but it is useful to have a reminder of what it means and involves:

The professional ethics of an organisation are the moral principles or standards that govern the conduct of the members of that organisation.

The AAT has its own Code of Professional Ethics, which will be referred to in this chapter. The main aims of this Code are to:

■ set out the expected standard of professional behaviour

■ help protect the public interest

■ help to maintain the AAT's good reputation

This Code applies to AAT members in particular but the **five basic fundamental principles** set out in the Code can also be applied as a benchmark to the behaviour of all staff working in an accounting environment.

the five fundamental ethical principles

When you are carrying out your research for your Report, whether it is based on a real workplace or an AAT Case Study, you will need to distinguish between situations that **are ethical** and situations that **are not ethical**. You will have to evaluate all that you see going on in the accounting system and measure this behaviour against the AAT five fundamental ethical principles. It may be that the real or possible unethical situations involve just one principle, or they may involve a combination of principles.

The AAT's five fundamental ethical principles are:

1 **Integrity** – which involves honesty, truthfulness and fair dealing

2 **Objectivity** – not being influenced through conflicts of interest and bias

3 **Professional Competence and Due Care** – developing professional knowledge and skills, and using them to the full

4 **Confidentiality** – when to disclose information and when not to

5 **Professional Behaviour** – to act in a 'professional' way and not bring the profession into disrepute

We will cover these principles in detail in the first part of this chapter and show, using practical examples, how they can help you provide evidence for your Report.

INTEGRITY

When you say that someone is a person of 'integrity' it means that they are:

- **straightforward** and **honest** in their professional dealings:
    - they keep to the policies and procedures set down by the accounting function of the organisation
    - they do not take short cuts or allow anything to pass through the accounting system which they know has not been checked
    - they do not allow anything to pass through the accounting system which they know is incorrect or if something is missing
- **fair dealing** and **truthful** in their professional dealings:
    - they do not falsify or 'fudge' figures either for internal or external use, eg financial reports or sales figures
    - they do not intentionally mislead customers or suppliers with false information, eg prices, discounts

In short, a person who has integrity has high standards of conduct and expects high standards of colleagues. That person will not allow anything that is incorrect or misleading to pass through the accounting system.

breaches of integrity

When you are preparing your Report you will need to identify situations where the ethical principle of integrity in an accounting system **is** compromised, or **could be** compromised. You will need to provide recommendations for the action to be taken. Set out below is an example. Further examples are included in the Report Writing Hints on page 58.

situation

An accounting supervisor realises that sales figures supplied to a lending bank as part of the company's regular management accounts reporting have been inflated by the Accounts Manager. This means that the bank is consistently given a false indication of the company's financial position.

the ethical problem

This is a case of a lack of **integrity** in the company's management. They have been neither **honest** nor **truthful** in their professional dealings with the bank.

recommendation

This is a serious case and will have to be brought to the attention of the person to whom the Accounts Manager is responsible.

OBJECTIVITY

A person who is **objective** is a person who sticks to the facts and does not allow his or her decisions or actions to be affected by other people's opinions or influence.

In an accounting context there is the requirement that accounting staff should not have day-to-day professional or business decisions swayed by:

- **bias**, an unfair discrimination against somebody for a variety of reasons, for example:
  - their race, colour or gender
  - you just do not like them because you have had a disagreement with them in the past or you do not like their politics
- **conflict of interest**, a situation where your professional judgement is affected because you could benefit personally from a transaction, for example:
  - giving a customer favourable terms (discounts, payment periods) because you are relying on that customer for voting you onto a sports club committee
- **undue influence**, a situation where someone is putting undue pressure on you to do something that you do not consider professional, for example:
  - a manager promises to put you up for promotion if you keep quiet about the fact that you have found out that he puts in expense claims for when he takes his girlfriend out for meals

When you are preparing your Report you will need to identify situations where the ethical principle of objectivity in an accounting system could be called into question, as in the example below. See also page 58.

situation

An accounting assistant working in Credit Control sees that one customer who is behind with paying his account has not been sent a chaser letter on two occasions. You happen to know that this customer is a good friend of the Accounts Manager and that they regularly play golf together.

the ethical problem

This is potentially a case of a breach of **objectivity** on the part of the Accounts Manager: there is a **conflict of interest** in his dealings.

recommendation

This case will need to be verified. The assistant could mention to his line manager that the two letters had not gone out; it may be a mistake in the system. It would then be up to the line manager to take the matter further.

PROFESSIONAL COMPETENCE AND DUE CARE

Professional Competence means acquiring an appropriate level of knowledge and skills for working at a particular level in an accounting system. The more senior you are the more comprehensive and specialised the knowledge and skills will have to be.

Due Care means that the accounting professional must take the required level of care appropriate to the task undertaken, whether this is checking an invoice or preparing the financial statements of a business. In short, the individual must provide a competent and 'professional' service.

Professional Competence and Due Care requires the person working in an accounting environment to:

- plan career progression through **CPD** (**Continuing Professional Development**), a programme of development involving qualifications, internal courses and expanding experience which enable the individual to attain and maintain a **competent professional service**

- act **diligently** – this means carrying out a task according to instructions, carefully, thoroughly and on time

- exercise **sound judgement** in applying professional knowledge and skills and knowing their limitations

- know when to **decline to carry out an area of work** (eg payroll processing) if the person does not have the necessary knowledge or skills; in other words, to recognise the limits of his or her professional competence

The example below illustrates this ethical principle. See also page 58.

situation

You are an accounting assistant working in the Sales Ledger section of the accounting system of a large company. You have been asked by your line manager to prepare the data for the online quarterly VAT Return, something you have never done before. The line manager says 'You have covered this in your studies. I am sure you will be OK' and walks out.

the ethical problem

This is a problem of **Professional Competence and Due Care**. You have no experience in this area and will be unable to carry out this task to the required level of professional competence.

recommendation

You will have to find and speak to your line manager and explain the situation. Tell her diplomatically that you cannot undertake the task and maybe ask her for some training in that area.

CONFIDENTIALITY

Confidentiality is the duty not to disclose information about another person or organisation (eg customers of a business, clients of an accounting firm) which is given or obtained during the normal course of business, unless . . .

- the person or organisation involved (the subject of the information) gives **consent** for the release of the information, to an auditor, for example

- there is a **legal duty** to disclose information, eg in the case of suspected money laundering

- the disclosure is in the **public interest**, eg a client who appears to be involved in or funding terrorist activities

Breaches of confidentiality can occur in other contexts:

- information should not be given in a **social context**, eg gossip at the golf club or in the local gym or club

- information should not be shared with family members

- information should not be given by employees to third parties after they have left the employer for another job

situation
One of your colleagues is in the office chatting to a customer on the phone. You overhear her say that one of your other customers is having cash flow problems and has sold his Porsche.

the ethical problem
This is a breach of **Confidentiality**. The information your colleague has given to the other customer could seriously damage the credit standing of the customer having liquidity problems.

recommendation
This is a situation which should be covered in a company Guidance on Confidentiality document. You should bring this to your colleague's attention. If there is no document, you should suggest that one is drawn up.

PROFESSIONAL BEHAVIOUR

Professional Behaviour is an ethical principle which requires people working in accounting to comply with the laws and regulations that relate to the accounting profession. They also need to uphold the good reputation of the profession and its individual members. Examples of breaches of the professional behaviour principle include:

- individuals making false claims about their professional competence, for example:

- falsifying a CV, eg claiming to have qualifications they do not possess
- claiming they have competence in a particular area when their knowledge is very limited

▨ individuals making disparaging remarks about other members of the profession

▨ bringing the profession into disrepute, for example an accountant being involved in a serious highly publicised fraud case

---

situation

An accounts assistant gets a job on the basis of claiming that he had an AAT qualification when in fact he was not yet qualified.

the ethical problem

This is a clear breach of **Professional Behaviour**. The claim of professional competence is false and could cost him his job.

recommendation

There is no immediate solution to this situation, except for the person to finish his qualification and then apply for accounting jobs.

REPORT WRITING HINTS – PROFESSIONAL ETHICS

Set out below are some situations in which professional ethics are compromised. They should help you to look for similar situations to include in your Report. You should always treat such situations with great **sensitivity**.

- **integrity**
  - taking money from the petty cash and not recording the withdrawal
  - falsifying inventory records to hide pilferage of stock

  These are both also examples of **fraud** in the workplace.

- **objectivity**
  - giving extra discount to a customer who has given you football tickets
  - refusing extended credit to a customer because you do not agree with his politics

- **professional competence and due care**
  - forgetting to take credit references on a new customer
  - not completing the necessary documentation for casual workers

- **confidentiality**
  - leaving employee pay slips (not in envelopes) in the office in-tray
  - giving an unknown caller the telephone number of an employee

- **professional behaviour**
  - telling a customer that one of your colleagues is 'useless'
  - your employer advertises tax advice as one of its services when none of its employees is qualified to provide it

SUSTAINABILITY – THE BACKGROUND

'**Sustainability**' is a term that is widely and loosely used to describe the need for organisations and individuals to adopt 'green' policies which protect the environment, save energy and benefit society.

When preparing for your project you will need to evaluate an accounting system to see how 'sustainable' it is, and how it might be improved. In order to approach this aspect of your Report preparation in an organised way it is important to appreciate the origin and exact meaning of the term 'sustainability' and its wider implications. It is important to realise that sustainability also involves a number of economic and social issues.

some history

In the mid-1980s Gro Harlem Brundtland, a former Norwegian Prime Minister, headed the **Brundtland Commission**, an independent international body set up by the UN to tackle the problems of increasing worldwide environmental damage caused by unrestricted profit-driven businesses. The result of the Commission was the **Brundtland Report**, published in 1987.

The objective of the Commission was to persuade governments worldwide to limit environmental damage while at the same time encouraging responsible economic growth which would benefit society in general – both at that time and also in the future. This idea of 'sustainable development' was defined in the Brundtland Report in general terms as follows:

'**Sustainable development is development that meets the needs of the present without compromising the ability of future generations to meet their own needs.**'

This definition of sustainability was further refined by the identification of three main objectives, described below.

the 'three pillars' of sustainability

The three main objectives (the 'pillars') of sustainable development are:

■ economic growth
■ environmental protection
■ social equality

These are sometimes also referred to as the 'triple bottom line' of financial, environmental and social factors, or simply 'profit, planet and people' – which is a rough and ready way of remembering the three main objectives. These objectives are explained in more detail in the pages that follow.

the 'Three Pillars' of Sustainable Development

economic growth and sustainability

Economic growth is important because it makes sustainable development possible. The term 'economic growth' relates to:

■ the growth of the economies of individual countries leading to wealth creation which benefits the whole population

■ the generation of profit or surpluses by individual organisations that will bring financial benefits to owners, employees and the economy locally and nationally

It should be stressed that this economic growth should not be made at the expense of other sustainability factors, for example the undesirable profit-making, criticised by the Brundtland Report.

In your Report you could include examples of the use of economic growth such as:

■ using company profits to make donations to national charities

■ using company profits to support events in the local community

environmental protection and sustainability

The need to protect the environment and conserve resources – also known as the 'green' factor – is one that is most commonly associated with sustainability. Examples of 'green' policies include:

■ the use of power generated from 'free' sources such as wind and the sun

■ initiatives in the workplace to reduce the consumption of electricity, eg 'turn off that computer at night' campaigns

■ energy-saving devices such as LED and low-energy lights

- the use of recycled materials in the office, eg paper and printer toner cartridges
- reducing the 'carbon footprint', eg cycle to work schemes, the provision of low-emission company car sharing
- requiring businesses in the supply chain to certify their 'green' credentials, eg farmers supplying supermarkets being required to avoid the use of harmful pesticides

One of the major advantages of cutting down on the use of resources such as energy and consumables is that it can **save money**. This means that it actually pays a business to introduce 'green' policies. If a business runs a fleet of fuel-efficient company cars, it will reap the financial rewards of lower fuel costs and the tax benefits for using low emission vehicles.

Another example of money-saving through a 'green' policy is the practice adopted by some retailers of charging customers for plastic bags. This has the dual effect of providing extra income for the retailer while at the same time cutting the costs of providing bags – all to the benefit of the environment.

social equality and sustainability

This factor concentrates on the social well-being of people, not just in one locality, but worldwide. At the time of writing there is a distinct lack of equality and well-being. It is estimated that

- 1% of the world's population owns 40% of the world's wealth
- 1% of the world's wealth is owned by the poorest 50% of the world's population

These figures speak for themselves, and it does credit to the social consciences of individuals and organisations that the UK-based entertainment charity Comic Relief has at the time of writing raised over £800 million for causes in seventy countries worldwide. Comic Relief states on its website:

We spend that money in the best possible way to tackle the root causes of poverty and social injustice.

When preparing your Report there are various areas which you could investigate which will provide evidence for the organisation's accounting function being involved in helping society. For example:

- direct charitable donations to national charities which directly help the socially underprivileged, eg Comic Relief
- sponsorship of local charitable fund-raising events
- sponsorship of local sports events
- sponsorship of local arts events

An organisation can also provide social benefits in a more direct sense, for example:

- providing work experience in the workplace
- financially supporting an employee who is improving his or her skills by studying for a vocational qualification (eg AAT)

In these last two examples, the organisation will also benefit, both in helping their recruitment and also in improving the 'skill set' of its employees.

CORPORATE SOCIAL RESPONSIBILITY (CSR)

If the organisation you are investigating is a large one you may find that it has published a **Corporate Social Responsibility (CSR)** document. This will formalise and set out many of the aspects of sustainability that you are investigating. If the subject of your Report does not produce a CSR document, you may find it useful to study some examples from well-known companies. Try a web search on 'Tesco CSR Reports' or 'M&S CSR'.

The Tesco statement of strategy for sustainable development is set out below:

Our seven part strategy sets out clear goals for the business to ensure we deliver long-term sustainable growth. Putting our responsibilities to the communities we serve at the heart of what we do is an essential part of it. By operating responsibly and working with customers, suppliers, expert partners and NGOs our hope is that we can leave the world a better place; a greener, healthier and more prosperous place than when we began.

Examples of Corporate Social Responsibility (CSR) initiatives adopted by companies such as Tesco include:

- sourcing its products where possible from renewable resources and where local economies will benefit (eg 'Fair Trade' coffee and bananas)
- ensuring that the supply chain is also actively supporting sustainable development (environmentally and socially) and is treated with respect
- reducing CO_2 emissions from premises and from distribution networks
- staff and customer fundraising
- donation of a percentage of profits to charities and good causes
- providing comprehensive staff training and promotion prospects

Marks & Spencer are also active in promoting sustainable development and publish an annual 'How we do Business Report'. Their commitments are based around what they call 'Plan A' and include becoming carbon neutral, sending no waste to landfill, extending sustainable sourcing, setting new standards in ethical trading and helping customers and employees to live healthier lifestyles. An extract from a 'How we do Business Report' is shown below. The page references are to the 2012 Report, available for download from http://corporate.marksandspencer.com

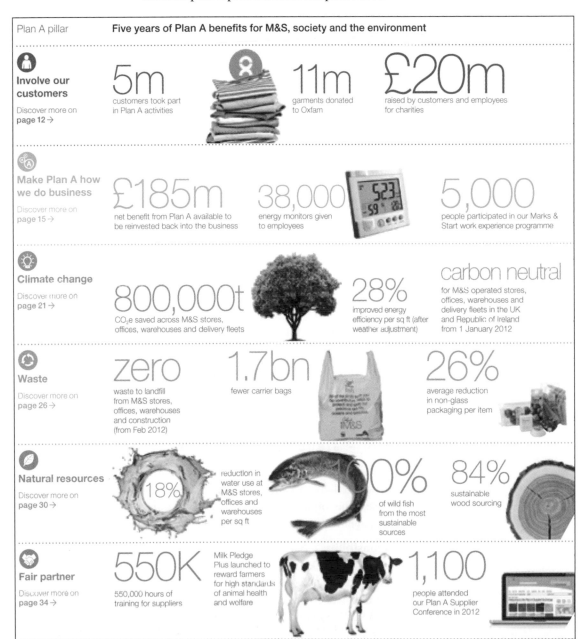

Plan A pillar	Five years of Plan A benefits for M&S, society and the environment
Involve our customers Discover more on page 12 →	**5m** customers took part in Plan A activities **11m** garments donated to Oxfam **£20m** raised by customers and employees for charities
Make Plan A how we do business Discover more on page 15 →	**£185m** net benefit from Plan A available to be reinvested back into the business **38,000** energy monitors given to employees **5,000** people participated in our Marks & Start work experience programme
Climate change Discover more on page 21 →	**800,000t** CO₂e saved across M&S stores, offices, warehouses and delivery fleets **28%** improved energy efficiency per sq ft (after weather adjustment) **carbon neutral** for M&S operated stores, offices, warehouses and delivery fleets in the UK and Republic of Ireland from 1 January 2012
Waste Discover more on page 26 →	**zero** waste to landfill from M&S stores, offices, warehouses and construction (from Feb 2012) **1.7bn** fewer carrier bags **26%** average reduction in non-glass packaging per item
Natural resources Discover more on page 30 →	**18%** reduction in water use at M&S stores, offices and warehouses per sq ft **100%** of wild fish from the most sustainable sources **84%** sustainable wood sourcing
Fair partner Discover more on page 34 →	**550K** 550,000 hours of training for suppliers Milk Pledge Plus launched to reward farmers for high standards of animal health and welfare **1,100** people attended our Plan A Supplier Conference in 2012

AAT and CSR

Another organisation which produces a Corporate Social Responsibility Policy is the AAT. This document can be downloaded by following the link: http://www.aat.org.uk/about-aat/aat-sustainability. The key principles of this document are shown below:

AAT recognises that its operations inevitably have an impact on wider environmental, economic and social issues. These issues are an integral part of our quality management process and we believe that placing emphasis on them gives the right message to our employees, members, suppliers and other key stakeholders and demonstrates our awareness of, and concern for, the wider community.

We are committed to continuous improvements in environmental, economic and social sustainability.

We will comply with all European law applicable to environmental legislation, regulations, approved codes of practice and other external requirements applicable to our business.

We will continuously develop our CSR policy by:

- measuring and reporting our performance
- identifying opportunities and taking action where practical to meet legal obligations and improve sustainability
- identifying adverse impacts and risks, and where possible mitigate these
- promoting our CSR policy and gain buy in from all our employees and other key stakeholders
- embedding our CSR policy and practice into all our management systems, standards, processes and procedures.

UK LEGISLATION AND INTERNATIONAL STANDARDS

You will not need a detailed knowledge of the legal requirements for aspects of sustainable development or of the recommended international standards, but you should be aware that there is a legal framework that regulates these areas. You may well come across these when researching for your Report.

UK legislation and regulations which affect the workplace and protect the environment include:

- Health & Safety at Work Act 1974 and the Clean Air Act 1993
- Waste Electronic and Electrical Equipment (WEEE) Regulations 2006, which aim to reduce the amount of WEEE being disposed of

ISO 26000 – standards for social responsibility

The **International Organisation for Standardisation** sets standards (**ISOs**) which are adopted by organisations worldwide and enables them to be certified when the organisations reach the required standard. ISO 9001 (Quality Management) is the most common of these standards.

Social responsibility – one of the 'pillars' of sustainable development – is covered by ISO 26000. It helps businesses and organisations operate in a socially responsible way, on a global scale. It must be noted that ISO 26000 only gives guidance; it does not award certification to organisations in the way that ISO 9001 (Quality Management) does.

REPORT WRITING HINTS – SUSTAINABILITY

For the part of your Report which deals with sustainability issues you will need to identify:

- areas where any of the three 'pillars' of sustainability are in evidence (ie economic growth, environmental protection, social equality)
- areas where aspects of sustainable development could be introduced

A good starting point for research is the Corporate Social Responsibility (CSR) document which the organisation might have produced.

Specific areas of sustainability which should be investigated include:

- **economic growth**
  - schemes for increasing sales and productivity, eg bonus schemes, profit-sharing, staff suggestion schemes
  - areas where resources can be managed efficiently so that costs can be cut and profitability increased (these are often in areas where the environment can be improved, eg recycling of materials, reduction of waste, energy economies)

- **environmental protection**
  - reducing the carbon footprint (eg using eco-friendly company cars, cutting down on unnecessary car journeys)
  - energy saving (eg turning off lights and computers when leaving work)
  - waste management (eg re-using toner cartridges and sending paper and other waste for recycling)
  - using materials from sustainable resources (eg books, such as this one, printed on paper manufactured from forests which are being replanted rather than being depleted)
  - using suppliers who also have proven sustainability policies

- **social equality**
  - charitable giving on a local, national and international scale
  - sponsorship of national and local sports events (eg marathons)
  - sponsorship of national and local arts events (eg local school productions)
  - valuing and developing the workforce (eg financing an employee's AAT course and giving time off for study)
  - providing work experience to school and college students
  - providing prizes for school and college award ceremonies

5 Reviewing accounting systems and making recommendations

this chapter covers...

In this chapter we look at the issues involved in reviewing an accounting system and making recommendations for improvement.

The review will involve assessing the strengths of the accounting system:

- seeing how it fulfils the needs of the organisation and the wider community
- seeing how effective the internal control system is in terms of procedures, communication and training

The review will then assess the weaknesses of the accounting system, analysing

- weaknesses in the internal control system
- the possibilities for error and fraud involving the loss of money, inventory and reputation
- the possibilities for breaches of professional ethics
- ways in which sustainable development policies can be introduced or improved

The chapter then explains the need to make recommendations for improvement to the accounting system in each area of weakness. This includes analysis of:

- the likely changes needed and the training needs
- the costs involved in each recommendation and the likely benefits that will follow

We look at the way in which these recommendations will impact on the staff involved:

- the help and training that they will need
- the benefits of various computer systems

WHAT ARE YOU GOING TO REVIEW?

Before you start your review of an accounting system it is important to know exactly what you are going to review. This will depend on a number of factors:

the method of assessment

You will either be basing your investigation on

■ **workplace evidence**, or

■ an **AAT Case Study**

If you have chosen to base your assessment on **evidence from an actual workplace**, your choice of area of investigation will largely depend on the size of the organisation. This issue is explained in the next section.

If you chose an **AAT Case Study** (see pages 98-115 for a sample) you are given a scenario of an accounting system – with all its many problems and shortcomings – to analyse and make recommendations. You can analyse the whole system or you can choose just one or more of the accounting functions for analysis.

the size of the organisation

If the organisation is large, say a large company or public sector organisation, the accounting system may also be large and departmentalised. To review the whole system will be an immense task and you are recommended to chose one or two parts of it, eg payroll or sales ledger. As your investigation will then be limited in breadth, you will need to research in greater depth.

If, on the other hand, the organisation is smaller, a family business for example, you are likely to need to take a wider view of the accounting system. It is very possible that the system in this case is operated by a limited number of people who each take on a number of the various accounting functions such as payroll, sales ledger and cashiering. In this situation your review is likely to cover more of the accounting roles.

The main functional areas required for an accounting system have already been mentioned in Chapter 2. They include:

■ the individual ledgers: purchases ledger, sales ledger and nominal ledger

■ credit control

■ cash handling and banking

■ petty cash

■ payroll

■ budgeting and management reporting

review contents and method – an overview

An accounting system review is likely to cover the following areas:

- The accounting **records** and financial **reports** extracted from the records: are they sufficient and do they provide the necessary information?
- The **internal control systems**: how efficient are they in detecting and preventing fraud and in following the requirements of **ethical practice**?
- **Methods of working**: eg use of computers, how reliable and fast are they? Are they used in a cost-effective way? To what extent does the need for **sustainability** affect working practices?
- How well are the staff **trained** and provided with CPD opportunities?

In short, the review will assess the **strengths** of the existing system – in terms of its internal control system, cost-effectiveness, reliability and speed. It will also carry out an analysis of the **weaknesses** of the existing system, giving you grounds for your recommendations for improvement.

You may find it useful to draw up a SWOT analysis, although this should not be included in the review.

IDENTIFYING THE STRENGTHS OF THE SYSTEM

There are various areas of investigation which will indicate how effective the accounting system is in preventing errors and deterring fraud. You could:

- draw up an organisational chart of the accounting system showing the areas of responsibility and the various reporting lines; process flow charts are also very useful in showing the way the system works
- identify the other operational areas of the organisation which it supports

You can then investigate in more detail the internal control system to see how reliable it is. You can ask questions which relate to a number of different aspects of internal control:

operating procedures, reliability and efficiency?

'Is there a Policies and Procedures (or similar) document?'

'Is the authorisation system for payments clear and workable?'

'Are there the necessary routine checking procedures in place?'

'Are there random checks made to ensure procedures are being followed correctly?'

'Are the records kept in an organised way?'

'Are passwords (both to computers and premises) kept secure and changed when necessary?'

'Are items such as the petty cash box and the company cheque books kept under lock and key and are the keys kept only by authorised staff?'

'Are the reporting lines within the organisation working efficiently?'

'Is the system cost-effective – does it use resources efficiently?'

'Is there a sustainability policy in operation, eg a 'cycle to work' scheme, recycling of materials and a power-saving initiative?'

'Are there safeguards to ensure ethical behaviour, eg confidentiality guidelines?'

'Is the system completely reliable, eg if staff are away?'

computer systems?

A well-organised accounting system should ideally have an integrated computer system on a network using proprietory software such as Sage and Microsoft Office. This will enable accounting staff to input and access their own accounting data and also have access to other data kept in the system – subject to passwords and authorisation, of course.

A well-developed computer system will also help when new or temporary staff are brought in and have to get used to the organisation's routine and procedures at short notice.

staff training?

An effective accounting system will operate well if the staff are well-trained in a range of processes and are multi-skilled. This is especially true of a small business where staff have to cover for colleagues who are off sick, on holiday, or on maternity leave. As we will see later in this chapter, training comes at a cost and will need to be able to repay the investment.

All these aspects of a well-developed accounting system contribute to its **strength**. It is when the system fails in some or all of these areas that **weaknesses** appear and errors and fraud can then occur.

IDENTIFYING THE WEAKNESSES OF THE SYSTEM

The weaknesses in an accounting system often result in **errors** or in **fraud**.

errors

Errors result from inefficiencies in the internal control system and can cause all sorts of problems, for example:

- an invoice being sent to the wrong customer
- a discount being incorrectly calculated

- a payment to a supplier being made very late
- an employee being paid the wrong rate of pay
- a customer being sent a formal demand for an overdue account when in fact payment has already been received but entered to the wrong account

You will doubtless be able to add other examples to this list of unfortunate accidents. What these examples have in common is that they result in some form of loss to the organisation involved:

- **loss of money** – when a payment is made for the wrong amount or a discount is incorrectly calculated
- **loss of time** – when a problem has to be sorted out and emails and apologies sent – time is also money, of course
- **loss of reputation** – when customer expectations are not met and the organisation loses face – and even its customer's business

fraud

Fraud, which was covered in detail in Chapter 3, is another consequence of basic weaknesses in the internal control system of an organisation. It also poses a threat of loss:

- **loss of money** – monetary-based frauds include purchase ledger staff paying fictitious suppliers and diverting the money to their own account, or payroll staff using the same principle to send payroll payments to fictitious employees
- **loss of inventory** – for example, a case of an employee over-ordering valuable inventory and then stealing it and arranging for its sale at a nearby street market
- **loss of time** – employees overstating time worked on time sheets

It is probably unlikely that you will uncover any major frauds when basing your assessment on workplace evidence, but you should write about the possible causes of fraud and the ways in which fraud can be prevented.

fraud and professional ethics

The incidence of **fraud** is closely related to the concept of professional ethics which you also have to evaluate. You will need to identify any areas of weakness in the professional ethics of the organisation and link them to the relevant fundamental ethical principles, for example:

- **organisational culture** – this means the attitude of everyone in the business to ethics; if the management does not care about the occasional 'fiddle' going on, the rest of the employees are likely to adopt the same attitude and the incidence of fraud will become more common; in this case the fundamental principle of **integrity**

■ **reporting structure** – if there is an inefficient reporting structure, an employee may not be able to report a breach of professional ethics to a more senior employee and the breach will go unnoticed by management

sustainability

The accounting system should be analysed to see if there are any practices which could prevent the organisation from complying with the three principles of sustainability: economic, environmental and social – eg

■ lack of control over power usage, eg no notices instructing staff to turn off computers and lights at the end of the day

■ unnecessary printing out and reading of financial reports which could be distributed electronically and viewed onscreen

practical examples of weaknesses

The AAT Case Study route to assessment will inevitably provide situations which illustrate weaknesses in an accounting system. The examples of situations quoted below are taken from a sample Case Study. Suggestions are made on the next page for the weaknesses they expose in the internal control system of the accounting function.

---

security codes

Access to the accounts office is gained through a keypad code, the code for which is UOYAB (Bayou – the boss's name – read backwards). This code is relatively common knowledge throughout the company as it is also the alarm code for the building, and is used by the warehouse store supervisors and manager when they close up in the evenings. When the computer system was set-up a password was installed to protect the work. This is also UOYAB, as John uses the same security code for everything throughout the company because he feels this makes life easier.

cash and banking

Banking is carried out on a Monday and Thursday, and this is normally Gary's job which he does during his lunch break. The Thursday banking of cash is often lower as John has now started to reduce the cheques drawn for wages by the amount of cash available in the office safe on a Thursday morning. His idea is that any cash available can be used to supplement the making up of the wages to reduce the amount of cash needed to be drawn from the bank. There is no petty cash system as such. If cash is needed for any incidental expenses, it is taken from the till floats and a note put in the till to cover this.

payroll

Jo had booked two weeks holiday over Christmas, as she wanted to spend this time with Harry. As she knew that she is the only member of staff who can operate the Sage payroll system she decided to complete three weeks pay packets on the same date – all based on the hours worked in the current week. She completed the pay packets and placed them in the safe, informing the supervisors that Gary will give them out on the correct Friday and that any over or under payments will be adjusted during the following week after she has returned to work.

POSSIBLE WEAKNESSES IN THE ACCOUNTING SYSTEM (see the situations on the previous page)

security codes

The password system in this organisations is very lax:

1   The password is easily worked out and remembered because it is the boss's name spelt backwards.

2   The same password is used for a variety of different purposes.

3   There is no indication that the password is ever changed.

4   There is open opportunity for fraud: the code is used for the warehouse store by the supervisors and manager when they lock up. Theft of inventory is easily possible.

cash and banking

The accounting system's arrangements for cash handling and recording of cash payments seems to be non-existent:

1   There is no petty cash system.

2   There appears to be no checking system for cash counting.

3   Cash is passed from the tills to the safe to the payroll assistant with no record of any kind being made of the transactions.

4   No accounting entries appear to reflect the movements in cash.

5   There is an open invitation to theft.

payroll

The payroll system has a number of weaknesses:

1   Only one person in the organisation is trained to operate Sage payroll.

2   Working out wages by guesswork without using timesheets is unacceptable practice.

3   To estimate future wage packets on one week's figures is also unacceptable practice.

4   There is apparently no consideration given to the PAYE implications of these estimates and potential amendments.

MAKING THE RECOMMENDATIONS

The review of the organisation's accounting system will have revealed:

■ the **strengths** of its internal control system and its method of operating

■ the **weaknesses** of the system and the consequent errors that occur and opportunities for fraud that exist

■ areas of strength and weakness relating to ethical and sustainability issues

Whether you are basing your Report on workplace evidence or on the AAT Case Study you will now need to:

■ make recommendations for improvement

■ justify those recommendations

As noted earlier in this chapter, if you are dealing with a **large organisation** you may have restricted your investigation to a single area and found a single area of weakness, for example the need to computerise a manual system. If this is the case you should be making two or three separate recommendations for improvement – eg various different computer system solutions – and weighing up the advantages and disadvantages of each.

If on the other hand you have investigated a **small organisation**, you are likely to be taking an overview of the whole accounting system and you will probably have identified and assessed a number of areas for improvement. In this case you should be providing a recommendation for each weakness.

> **Report writing hint**
>
> When you are investigating the weaknesses of an internal control system, make sure that what you are taking on is realistic. If you have identified a number of weaknesses (if it is a small business, for example) you should provide a recommendation for each one. If you are concentrating on a single area of weakness (eg inventory control in a large warehouse) you should provide a number of recommendations (eg different inventory control systems), comparing them for their advantages and disadvantages.

the importance of the computer system

One aspect of your review and recommendations is the importance of the computer system. It may be that the accounting system uses a variety of different computers which are standalone machines, possibly with different operating systems, using different software for the same purpose. It is possible that the accounting system only uses computers for some of the accounting functions, for example invoicing but not for payroll. It is even possible that the accounting system does not use computers at all!

The ideal set-up is likely to be a system:

■ that uses similar or identical computers, all with the same operating system

■ linked on a network

■ using the same software (loaded with the same version), eg Sage for accounting transactions and payroll, and Microsoft Office (Word, Excel, Access) for processing text, spreadsheets and database records

A further example taken from a sample AAT Case Study assessment is a typical example of an accounting system that is deficient in this respect and obviously needs bringing up-to-date:

---

computers

These are all run on a stand-alone basis, though they are all linked to the same printer.

Gary has designed a form in Microsoft Office Word which he uses as a pro-forma for invoicing.

Gary allows two half days per month for the task of telephoning customers who are late in paying; drawing the information from an aged trade receivables listing which has been set up on the Excel system to indicate customers whose accounts are outstanding for more than sixty days.

Jo had booked two weeks holiday over Christmas, as she wanted to spend this time with Harry (her son). As she knew that she is the only member of staff who can operate the Sage payroll system she decided to complete three weeks pay packets on the same date – all based on the hours worked in the current week.

There are **many weaknesses** in the computer system of this business:

■ the computers are stand-alone and so cannot link up with each other for data interchange

■ invoicing is carried out on a Word pro-forma rather than on a dedicated computer accounting program

■ the Aged Trade Receivables Schedule is drawn up on Excel, which means all the figures need to be entered manually – a very time-consuming operation

■ only one employee knows how to use Sage Payroll which leads to some very unconventional accounting practices!

In your **recommendations for improvement** you could suggest that a new computer system could be established with the following features:

- a network of computers using the same software, possibly Microsoft Office (or a suitable alternative)
- the acquisition of a Sage accounting package (eg Sage 50, or a suitable alternative) which will:
  - integrate with Sage Payroll
  - handle the invoicing
  - deal with the Nominal, Sales and Purchase ledgers
  - produce an Aged Trade Receivables Schedule (or be configured to export data to Excel)
  - require staff training in Sage and Microsoft Office

impact on the staff

A new or updated computer system or any significant change in the accounting system will clearly impact on the staff involved. They will feel challenged, and perhaps threatened.

Part of any recommendation for change should include a plan for ensuring that the staff will acquire the necessary skills and knowledge so that they can use the revised system effectively. This could include:

- internal training courses and external training courses
- 'teach-yourself' facilities such as manuals, DVDs, online tutorials and the 'Help' menus provided with the computer software
- telephone support lines made available by the software provider (Sage, for example, provide an excellent 'helpline')

Staff training can be an expensive item and should form a prominent element in the cost-benefit analysis (see below) which assesses the total costs of a recommendation against the benefits provided.

Not all recommendations for improvement of the accounting system will necessarily involve computers. Recommendations may include other modifications to the internal control system which will impact on staff because they will change everyday working processes. For example:

- improvements to checking procedures, eg supplier invoices paid
- improvements to authorisation procedures, eg sending of BACS payments and Faster Payments to suppliers
- increased security of cash handling, eg having two people to check tills
- increased password security, eg changing passwords regularly
- stricter procedures relating to confidentiality (a fundamental ethical principle)

All of these changes would need to be communicated to staff, incorporated in the operating instructions (Procedures) of the accounting system, and monitored on a regular basis. This too will cost money.

Lastly, there are also changes that will be brought about by implementation of '**sustainability**' policies, eg 'cycle to work' schemes, subsidised public transport and energy-saving programmes. All this will require planning and implementation.

HOW MUCH WILL IT ALL COST? – COST-BENEFIT ANALYSIS

Cost-benefit analysis compares the amount of resources used (which are measured in money terms) with the benefits obtained from a project (which are not always measurable in money terms).

what are the costs?

Cost-benefit analysis involves analysing and quantifying the potential costs of implementing an improvement in the accounting system. For example. there may be extra costs incurred in employing more staff, in staff training and acquiring new computer systems.

On the 'benefit' side you will need to analyse the benefits from a project that cannot be measured in financial terms, for example:

■ better communication links between staff

■ an improvement in the quality of a service provided to clients/customers

■ a more effective reporting system

Cost-benefit analysis tells you whether the benefits will outweigh the costs.

cost-benefit analysis – a practical example

Installation of a new computer system in the Accounts Department

An estimate of the likely costs is as follows:

	£
– the cost of the hardware	50,000
– the cost of the software	10,000
– the installation cost	2,500
– the cost of training the staff	3,790
– annual maintenance cost	1,750
– insurance of hardware and for loss of data	1,250
	69,290

When working out a statement of costs you should show how you arrived at the **training costs**. These costs include the cost of the time spent training by the employees of the organisation which would otherwise have been spent in productive work. A typical calculation might look like this:

time spent by a manager in training	£
20 hours x £50 per hour	1,000
plus 15% on employer costs	
(National Insurance etc)	150
time spent by 8 assistants in training	
20 hours x 8 x £10 per hour	1,600
plus 15% on employer costs	
(National Insurance etc)	240
time spent by external trainer	
20 hours x £40 per hour	800
TOTAL TRAINING COST	3,790

assessing the benefits

You may well ask 'How can these costs benefit the organisation?'

Sometimes the benefit will result in cost savings, although this is difficult to quantify and would not be expected in your recommendations

A new computerised system means that money savings can be made in the way the system operates, for example:

- many routine operations will be speeded up which will save time and therefore reduce the wages bill

- electronic statements of account to customers will save on postage

- electronic payments to suppliers will also save time and money

- computer printed invoices will have fewer errors and therefore save time and money

There are also benefits which cannot be quantified in terms of money:

- the organisation will appear more professional

- the service provided by the organisation will be more efficient, which means that there will be fewer errors and problems, all of which cost time and money

conclusion

In conclusion, you will see that the benefits which emerge from a cost-benefit analysis cannot always be given a monetary value. The final decision must rest on the evidence of all the benefits provided – in basic terms "will it significantly improve the accounting system and is it worth all the money?"

Report writing hint

When you make a recommendation for an improvement in an accounting system you should always carry out a cost-benefit analysis, giving a monetary value to the costs wherever possible.

If you cannot work out an exact cost an approximation is better than not quoting a cost at all.

inspiration page – for your notes

6 Writing the Report

this chapter covers...

This chapter offers practical advice on the writing of the Report. It covers:

■　　*the context of the Report in the assessment process*

■　　*the structure of the Report – the sections that it contains*

■　　*the writing process – keeping to approximately 4,000 to 5,000 words*

■　　*the writing style to be used*

■　　*the contents of the various sections of the Report*

■　　*establishing a plan and a time schedule for the Report*

■　　*the individual responsibilities of the student, assessor and workplace mentor (if the Report is based on a real workplace)*

THE REPORT AND THE ASSESSMENT PROCESS

The 4,000 to 5,000 word Report is the evidence for assessment of the 'Internal control and accounting systems' Unit. The timescale after teaching has ended is a maximum of **six months** allowed for completing the Report and the assessment process. This six months is made up of:

- **four months** for completing the writing of the Report after teaching has finished
- a further **two months** for any resubmissions (up to four are allowed)

workplace evidence or AAT Case Study?

The Report can be written on the basis of workplace evidence or an AAT Case Study.

If you base your Report on **workplace evidence**, as opposed to the AAT Case Study, you need a signed declaration from the workplace management – an '**authenticity statement**' which confirms that the Report is your own original work. This applies if you are in employment or are just an observer of the workplace and not actually on the payroll.

If the Report is based on an **AAT Case Study**, AAT requires an authenticity statement from the assessor confirming that the Report is the student's own work.

the need for mapping

To complete the assessment you will need to show that you have covered all the areas of assessment – the **assessment criteria** (see pages 12-13). This is done by completing a **mapping document** (see pages 14-15). If you have not covered all the assessment criteria in your Report you will need to provide in an Appendix to the Report a statement explaining the missing areas.

STRUCTURE OF THE REPORT – AN OVERVIEW

The Report should be presented in standard **report format**. A summary of a report format is shown on the next page. It is based on the format recommended by the AAT in its Study and Assessment Guide.

We will cover the required writing style in detail later in this chapter. All you need to appreciate at this point is that a report is a formal document and not an informal 'what I did' narrative. It should be formal in structure, in page layout and in its language.

SUGGESTED REPORT FORMAT AND CONTENTS

title page	a statement of what the Report is about, quoting your student name and membership number
list of contents	a full list of all the Report sections with page references
terms of reference	why the Report is being written – to cover the Unit 'Internal Control and Accounting Systems' and also to recommend improvements to an accounting system
executive summary	a short summary of the Report's findings and the benefits to the organisation of following its recommendations; this is designed to be read by the management of the organisation concerned
introduction	a factual summary of what the organisation does, its products, customers, suppliers and stakeholders, together with an overview of the accounting system and how it relates to other parts of the organisation and complies with external regulations
accounting system review	a detailed review of the accounting system (or a chosen part of it) covering record keeping systems, working methods, internal control systems, fraud protection, training and issues relating to professional ethics and sustainability
weaknesses identified	an analysis of the accounting system describing areas of weakness identified in the system review (ie in the previous section) and explaining how these weaknesses could affect the organisation
recommendations	possible solutions to all the area(s) of weakness identified (including weaknesses relating to ethics and sustainability), setting out the choice of the preferred courses of action and an implementation plan
cost-benefit analysis	an assessment of the cost of at least one of the proposed changes in relation to the benefits received
appendices	extra material such as organisation charts, questionnaires and other supporting documents; this is also the place for supporting statements to cover assessment criteria not covered in the Report
mapping	cross referencing to the assessment requirements of the Report by paragraph number

HINTS ON THE WRITING PROCESS

what is 4,000 to 5,000 words?

The target length of your Report is 4,000 to 5,000 words. You will be relieved to hear that this does not require a very long report. A normal full page might contain 500 words on average, so 4,000 to 5,000 words, for example, will fill eight to ten pages of normal word-processed text. You should aim for the equivalent of eight pages. Note that the final Report may be longer because each section starts on a new page. The word limit does not include the appendices, so you are free to include as much supporting material as you need, but it must be relevant and you must take care to avoid any breaches of confidentiality if you include copies of internal documents and accounting data.

word-processed format

The Report should be produced on the computer because it has to be submitted online. Word-processing programs will also enable you to carry out editing, produce tables and also make regular spellchecks and word counts. Also note that:

- the sections (eg 'Terms of Reference' and 'Executive Summary') should all start on a new page
- the sections and the paragraphs should be numbered; eg if 'Executive Summary' is Section 2, the paragraphs in that Section will be numbered 2.1, 2.2, 2.3, and so on

writing style

A formal report requires straightforward written English. There is nothing particularly difficult about producing written English; the problems lie with the current tendency to write as you speak, or as you text, or as you email. The result is often an abbreviated form of written English which as you will appreci8 does nt work 2 well on the page.

Another problem facing people who are not used to writing formal written English is that they think of it as some sort of overblown 'posh' sounding language which has to be complicated and impressive to make its point. Nothing could be further from the truth. The test of good written English is that it should be:

- plain and simple
- to the point
- understandable by a twelve year-old

You possibly think that the last point is some form of a joke, but you might be surprised to learn that quality newspapers aim for this level of reading ability. To sum up, the first rule of writing is 'keep it simple'. Good writing must be clear. Use short sentences. Get the message across.

hints on writing plain English in a report

- use **simple words** instead of complicated ones

- use **short sentences** instead of long ones

- use the **active tense** rather than the passive, eg 'the line manager *carries out* regular checks on the petty cash book' rather than 'regular checks *are carried out* on the petty cash book by the line manager'

- use the **third person** (he, she, they) rather than 'I' or 'we' – remember that the Report should be a formal analysis rather than 'this is what I think about . . .'

- **avoid slang** eg 'the line manager really *hacked off* the rest of the staff''; you should use the word 'annoyed' instead of 'hacked' to avoid the innocent reader assuming that some form of serious workplace injury had taken place

- avoid **abbreviations** such as 'isn't', didn't' and write the phrases in full: 'is not' and 'did not'

- avoid **jargon** and **acronyms** which may not be understood by the general reader, for example 'the FD disapproved of the BOGOF policy because it reduced margins' which means 'the Finance Director disapproved of the 'buy one, get one free' policy because it reduced margins'

other practical report writing hints

You may find that you will end up cutting material to keep within the word limit. Remember that the important material is your analysis of the accounting system and your recommendations for change. If you need to make cuts, they should be from the introductory sections which describe the organisation, its products, customers, suppliers and stakeholders.

Remember to back-up your work each time you work on your Report. There are too many sad stories such as 'I did my Report on my lap-top, but the hard disk corrupted and I lost the lot.'

Read what you have written. Print out copies of what you have done as you go along so that you can check your work.

Ask other people to read what you have written to make sure that the reader can understand your meaning. Your assessor will read what you write, but it is useful to ask a friend or a partner as well, as long as you do not endanger a serious relationship in the process.

SECTIONS OF THE REPORT

On the next few pages we will illustrate the various sections of the Report, all of which should start on a new page. We will explain what the headings mean and give an idea of what should be included in each section. Remember that report headings and formats are likely to vary from one organisation to another. The format shown here is the format favoured by the AAT, although the same basic structure should be common to any report.

You should adopt the format you are used to or a format given to you by your training provider. Alternatively, if you are not familiar with any format, you could adopt the format illustrated here.

title page

The title page should state:

- what the Report is about
- the purpose of the Report
- your name
- your AAT student membership number
- the date of submission

The title should *not* be 'Internal Control and Accounting Systems'.

An example is shown below.

An analysis of the manual accounting systems of Didgeree Limited with recommendations for conversion to a Sage 50 computer accounting system.

Submitted by: A S Tudent

AAT student membership number: N001999

Date: March 20xx

This Report is submitted for assessment of the AAT Unit 'Internal control and accounting systems'.

---

list of contents

The list of contents should list each section, including the appendices, in page order and give accurate page references.

Note that every section should start on a new page. This will mean, of course, that the Report will run to more than the number of pages (8 to 10) that 4,000 to 5,000 words will normally fill as solid text.

List of Contents

	page
Terms of reference	1
Executive summary	2
Introduction to Didgeree Limited	3
Accounting system review	5
Weaknesses in the accounting system	7

. . . and so on

---

terms of reference

The terms of reference outline the **reasons for writing the Report**. These are:

■ why the Report is required – ie it is part of your AAT assessment

■ the objectives of the Report set out by AAT – what you are hoping to achieve, ie recommend improvements to the accounting system

Note the use of paragraph numbering and bullet points to clarify the text.

---

1 Terms of Reference

1.1 This Report has been prepared to cover the assessment requirements of AAT Unit 'Internal control and accounting systems'.

1.2 The objectives of this Report are to:

• analyse the manual accounting system of Didgeree Limited in order to identify areas of weakness

• make recommendations for improving the accounting system through the introduction of a computerised system

---

executive summary

This is likely to be one of the last sections that you write. It is a report summary written for the senior (executive) management of the organisation involved. The object of the summary is to set out in a nutshell:

■ the analysis that took place – eg of a manual accounting system

■ the changes recommended to be made to the accounting system – eg through the computerisation of various sections of the accounting system, using Sage 50

■ a conclusion analysing the impact of the changes on the organisation – the benefits (speed, accuracy, better and up-to-date management information) outweighing the costs (hardware, software, training)

This summary need be no more than a page of text, presented in succinct paragraphs. Remember that the management reading the summary will be very familiar with the organisation (they manage it, after all) and will also be short of time!

introduction

This section is often the first part of the Report that you will write as it is easy to put together and will get rid of the blank sheet of paper syndrome.

What is required here is a brief description and overview of the organisation which is the subject of your Report. Details you could include are:

■ its name and location

■ legal status (eg limited company, local authority department, charity)

■ how long it has been functioning

■ what it does: its main 'products' and 'markets'

■ its customers

■ main competitors

■ its stakeholders (ie others who may have an interest of some kind in the organisation), eg the public, regulatory authorities, pressure groups

■ relevant external laws and regulations which affect its operations

■ structure of the organisation – where the accounting function fits in (you could include an organisation chart in the appendices)

Remember that this section is intended to 'set the scene' and should not be overburdened with too much detail. It should not be a history of the organisation.

Remember also that the Report is a report to management, and they will presumably know about most of what you include in this section. Clear paragraph numbering will help in this section, for example . . .

3   Introduction to Didgeree Limited

3.1   Didgeree Limited is a limited company, established in 1985 in Milburn, West Midlands.

3.2   Its main business is the importation and marketing of Australian giftware through its 'Boomerang' wholesale and mail order operations. Its customers are UK retail stores and mail order buyers. It has no significant UK competitor.

3.3   Its main stakeholders are the import regulatory authorities and environmental pressure groups who have objected to the sale of goods made from possum skins.

3.4   Didgeree Limited is organised into departments (including Accounting Department) – see Appendix 5 on page 22 for a structure chart.

accounting system review

This section should start with a description of the workings of the Accounting Department. A departmental structure chart (ie not the whole organisation) can be included in the Appendices. The details might include:

- the different sections of the Department, eg Purchases Ledger, Sales Ledger, Payroll and the approximate number of people employed
- where you fit into the Department (if you work in it)

But the important part of this section is your **analysis** of the Accounting system and the highlighting of weaknesses.

A useful starting point when you are planning this analysis is the SWOT approach. 'SWOT' is a traditional management analytical technique. The letters stand for **S**trengths, **W**eaknesses, **O**pportunities and **T**hreats.

Strengths   These are the 'plus' points of the accounting system and its management – for example an integrated computer accounting system which saves time and money, an efficient checking procedure and well trained staff.

Weaknesses   These are the areas that you will need to identify in order to carry out improvements to an out-of-date accounting system. They might include, for example, lack of training and insufficient staffing or obsolete computer hardware. These issues might open up the possibility of errors and fraud. There may also be weaknesses

Opportunities These are areas of an organisation (the accounting system in this case) which could be improved and developed and become the 'strengths', the 'plus' points. For example a manual accounting system could be computerised.

Threats Threats are external to the accounting system and could include possible outsourcing of accounting activities or a merger with another organisation.

Note: a SWOT analysis is a useful document for focusing your ideas on the strengths and weaknesses of an accounting system but it should **not** be included in the main body of the Report, but as an item in the Appendices.

Specific areas that should be covered in the review are:

- **record keeping systems** – the purpose of reports produced from accounting data – do they meet the needs of the organisation's various functions and management?

- **internal systems of control** – the types of internal control used within the accounting system – are they appropriate? are they sufficient? are they missing?

- **fraud** – coverage of the types and causes of fraud and the methods used to detect fraud – are there any potential areas for fraud within the organisation?

- **working practices** – areas including the use of appropriate computer software and hardware – are they reliable, efficient and cost effective?

- **training** – are staff sufficiently trained for the job?

- **professional ethics** – are there any actual or potential breaches of any of the five ethical principles of the AAT code?

- **sustainability** – how does the organisation rate when measured against the 'three pillars' of sustainable development – economic, environmental and social factors?

weaknesses identified

This part of the Report follows the accounting system review and identifies weaknesses in the system or areas where improvement could be made. Each weakness should be analysed and explained in depth, describing the effect it has on the organisation and its staff.

recommendations

For every weakness that has been identified there should be at least one recommendation made to rectify the situation. Recommendations are likely to include all aspects of the accounting system and all key features of the Report review section:

- record keeping systems
- internal systems of control and fraud
- working practices
- training
- professional ethics and sustainability

Note:

The area of the Report covering **weaknesses** and **recommendations** can be dealt with in two different ways:

1 as two separate sections, one (weaknesses) listing all the weaknesses followed by another section (recommendations) listing all the recommendations

2 as a single section 'weaknesses and recommendations' with every weakness identified being followed in the text by the appropriate recommendation

cost-benefit analysis

You should produce a cost-benefit analysis for at least one of the recommendations you have made. A cost-benefit analysis will quantify in money terms the costs of a proposal and weigh them against the potential benefits. See pages 76-78 for a worked example of a cost-benefit analysis for the introduction of a computerised accounting system.

appendices

Appendices comprise the information that supports the Report. They:

- are not included in the target word count of 4,000 to 5,000 words
- should be numbered
- should be relevant and cross-referenced in the text of the Report
- may include confidential material and so it is essential that the permission of the relevant organisation is given before material can be used

Examples of appendices include:

- structure charts of the organisation and its accounting system
- relevant financial documents, eg sample invoices, inventory records
- SWOT analysis
- internal memoranda and minutes of meetings
- questionnaires used and analysis of findings from the questionnaires
- statements to cover assessment criteria not covered in the main Report

As noted above, the appendices should be relevant and cross-refer to the text of the Report. Avoid the temptation to use the appendices as a dumping ground for excess material.

and do not forget . . . your letter of authenticity

If the Report is based on a real workplace you will need a letter from your workplace manager – a **letter of authenticity** – to authenticate your Report. The letter should state that the Report is all your own work and the confidentiality aspects have been covered.

The letter must be: on headed paper and dated and signed by the workplace manager, with his/her name and job title.

The text of an example letter of authenticity from a workplace is shown below. Note that if you are using an AAT Case Study for evidence, your assessor will provide an authenticity statement.

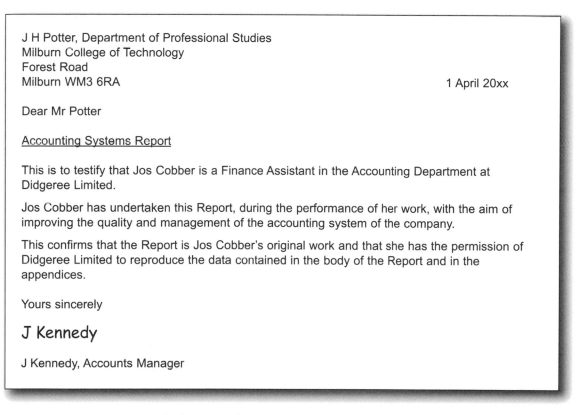

J H Potter, Department of Professional Studies
Milburn College of Technology
Forest Road
Milburn WM3 6RA   1 April 20xx

Dear Mr Potter

Accounting Systems Report

This is to testify that Jos Cobber is a Finance Assistant in the Accounting Department at Didgeree Limited.

Jos Cobber has undertaken this Report, during the performance of her work, with the aim of improving the quality and management of the accounting system of the company.

This confirms that the Report is Jos Cobber's original work and that she has the permission of Didgeree Limited to reproduce the data contained in the body of the Report and in the appendices.

Yours sincerely

J Kennedy

J Kennedy, Accounts Manager

and do not forget . . . mapping

An important document related to the completion of your assessment is the **mapping** carried out by you to make sure that all the assessment criteria have been covered, either in the Report itself or through statements in the Appendix. See Chapter 1 (pages 14 and 15).

TIME PLANNING

In the first chapter of this book we illustrated the processes needed for the successful completion of your Report, using the diagram reproduced on the next page. Efficient **time planning** is essential so that you can get going as soon as possible. You should be guided by your own training provider who will have planned a timetable for you, whether you use workplace evidence or the AAT Case Study for your evidence.

timetable for Report based on workplace evidence

Stage 1:
Learning

Decide on your subject – in discussion with your assessor and workplace mentor. During this period you will **study the theoretical areas** of organisations, accounting systems, internal control systems, fraud, professional ethics and sustainability, covering all the required assessment criteria.

Stage 2:
Writing

During the second stage you should **complete the first draft** of the complete Report, mapped to the assessment criteria, so that it can be sent online to your assessor. You have a maximum of **six months** for completing the assessment. This is made up of **four months** for the first draft to be submitted to your assessor and **two months** for a maximum of four resubmissions. You are likely to have **assessor consultations** to help you finalise the Report. If you find that there are assessment criteria that still need covering you will at this stage be able to prepare statements for inclusion in the Appendices. The final version can then be submitted to your assessor electronically.

timetable for Report based on an AAT Case Study

Stage 1:
Learning

As you will not have to worry about choosing a workplace, you should use this period of time to **study the theoretical areas** of organisations, accounting systems, internal control systems, fraud, professional ethics and sustainability, covering all the required assessment criteria. You should make yourself familiar with the **report format**.

Stage 2:
Writing

You will need to agree with your assessor whether you are analysing the whole or just a part of the accounting system described in the Case Study. You will again have six months to complete the assessment (four months for first draft, two months for up to four resubmissions). The whole process will involve assessor consultations and the final Report will be submitted to the assessor electronically.

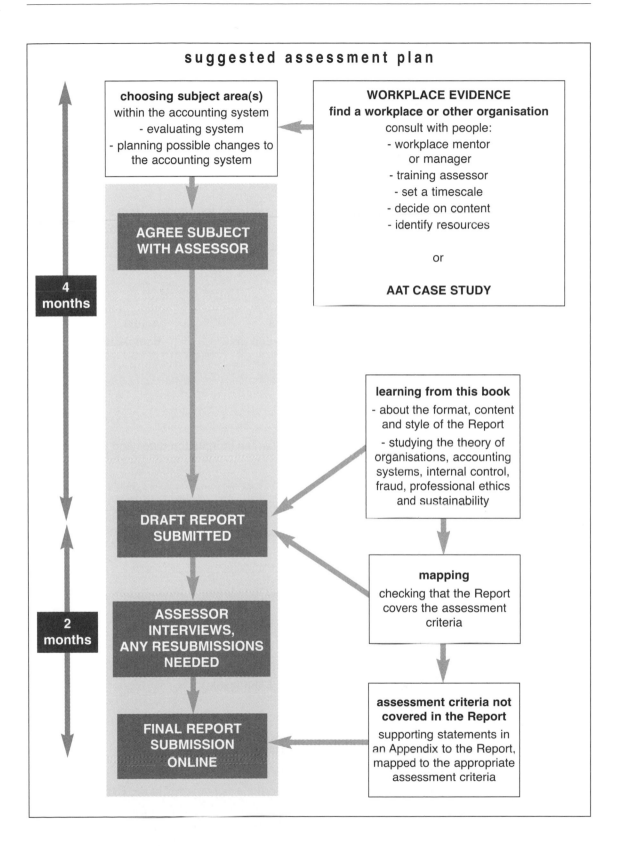

RESPONSIBILITIES FOR THE REPORT

Although it is the student who has to write the Report, it is important to appreciate that the responsibilities for its successful completion are shared with the assessor and, if workplace evidence is used, the workplace mentor/manager. The responsibilities for the Report are summarised below.

student responsibilities

Some teaching centres recommend that the student draws up a formal assessment plan setting out the various tasks and deadlines as agreed with the assessor. This plan is then signed by the student. A possible format is . . .

ASSESSMENT PLAN

Task	Planned completion date	Actual completion date

I confirm I have agreed to the planned completion dates and will do my best to meet them.

signed   ....

name   ....

date   ....

Tasks that could be listed in this plan include:
- choose the subject for the Report
- choose a workplace mentor (if applicable)
- complete research
- complete first draft
- map content against assessment criteria
- preliminary assessor interview
- dealing with any assessment criteria not covered in the Report

Further responsibilities of the student include:

■ meeting with the assessor at agreed times

■ liaising with the workplace mentor/manager when necessary

■ ensuring that any confidentiality issues have been sorted out

assessor responsibilities

The assessor's overall responsibility is to guide the student through the assessment process to a successful completion of the Report and the required evidence. Specific responsibilities to each student include:

■ planning a realistic assessment programme

■ agreeing the subject of the Report through one-to-one sessions with the student

■ monitoring the production of evidence and ensuring that it is the student's own work

■ checking the evidence against the requirements

■ carrying out a preliminary assessment interview based on the Report first draft

■ providing any additional assessment requirements that may be necessary to ensure that all the assessment criteria have been covered

■ assessing the Report final version

■ notifying the AAT (via Internal Verifier) of competent results

workplace mentor responsibilities

If you choose to write a report on an actual workplace, the workplace mentor – who may be your boss or a senior employee in the area you are investigating – fulfils an important role in helping you complete your Report. This person should:

■ help you initially identify the workplace problems which you will try to remedy through the recommendations in your Report

■ help you to obtain the evidence you need

■ if possible, read through what you have written

■ resolve any problems of confidentiality of information

■ authenticate your work (see page 91 for a sample authentication letter)

Report writing hints

1   Ensure that you have studied and understood the correct format for your Report. You are advised to follow the recommendations of AAT in its Guidance. This format is summarised on pages 81-82 and the individual sections explained on pages 85-90.

2   Make sure that you know in your own mind what the target of 4,000 to 5,000 words represents.

3   Ensure that you have access to a suitable word-processing package, that you can print out drafts of your work, submit them online to your assessor, and, very importantly, that you can back-up your work.

4   Construct a time plan or an assessment plan. Make sure that your deadlines are firmly in your mind.

5   Remember to start each new section on a new page.

6   Read through your own work regularly and ask yourself 'Is this written in simple English? Can it be easily understood?'

7   Ask other people to read through your own work and ask them the same questions: 'Is this written in simple English? Can it be easily understood?'

8   As you write your Report ensure that you are referencing it, as you go along, to the assessment criteria in the format suggested by your assessor.

9   Organise your appendices efficiently. Make references to them in the text where appropriate. Only include relevant material.

10   Arrange to party when you have completed your Report.

AAT Sample Case Study Assessment

This Sample Case Study has been produced by the Association of Accounting Technicians and is reproduced here with their kind permission.

COOKRIDGE AND COOKRIDGE CARPETS

This sample case study has been produced by the AAT to provide an example of the type of Case Study assessment that may be used to provide evidence for writing the Report.

ASSESSMENT TASKS

You have recently been employed as Senior Accounts Clerk for Cookridge & Cookridge Carpets. This is a full-time position, and the organisation is willing to support you finishing your AAT Level 4 studies by attending the local college on an evening.

The first job the directors have asked you to do is to review the accounting system, the effectiveness of its internal controls, and whether the culture of the organisation could be improved in terms of working ethically and their environmental sustainability.

You are then asked to make any recommendations for improvements that you feel are necessary. The directors know there are many weaknesses, but are uncertain as to how these should be managed.

To help you in this they have asked the accounts clerks to prepare some brief information about themselves, an overview of the accounting system, and also a list of events that have occurred over the previous few months. This information can be found in the company diary (see pages 110-115).

The directors have also suggested you review the following documents:

http://www.aat.org.uk/sites/default/files/assets/AAT_Code_of_Professional_Ethics.pdf

http://www.aat.org.uk/about-aat/aat-sustainability

You are required to produce **a business report** for Peter and John Cookridge. This should be approximately **4,000 to 5,000** words long. The report should be mapped to the learning outcomes and assessment criteria by paragraph number to ensure all criteria are covered. *Please see this textbook, pages 14 and 15.*

Task one
Review and evaluate the accounting system

The review and evaluation can be of the complete system or of one or more of the accounting functions, depending on your findings, but it must specifically cover the following points:

- Record keeping systems – explain the purpose of financial reports, and the suitability of the organisation's current reports to meet organisational needs.

- Internal systems of control – identify how internal control supports the accounting system, the types of internal control in place, and any controls that are missing.

- Fraud – explain the causes of fraud, common types of fraud, methods that can be used to detect fraud and potential areas for fraud within the organisation.

- Working methods/practices – review the working methods used, including the use of appropriate computer software, and the operating methods in terms of reliability, speed and cost effectiveness.

- Training – Identify how training is or can be used to support staff.

- An evaluation of the accounting system's professional ethics against the professional ethics code of AAT and the organisation; identifying actual or possible breaches of any of the five fundamental principles of the code of professional ethics. Examples of this could include breaches of confidentiality, integrity, professional behaviour, objectivity and professional competence.

- An evaluation of sustainability within the accounting system, identifying where improvements could be made. This should look at the impact that the organisation has on the environment, the economy or society. Examples of this could be to reduce the carbon footprint, reduce the use of natural resources (paper, electricity, petrol, etc) or improving corporate social responsibility.

The review should cover all aspects of the assessment criteria, as mapped above, when it can naturally be introduced into the report. If it cannot be covered in the report then it can be covered within a written explanation included in the appendix.

Whilst a SWOT analysis may be a good starting place, this should not be placed in the body of the report.

Task two
Conduct an ethical evaluation of the accounting systems

- Evaluate the accounting systems against ethical principles by reviewing working practices.

- Identify any actual or possible breaches of professional ethics.

Task three
Conduct a sustainability evaluation of the accounting systems

- Evaluate the accounting systems against sustainability principles by reviewing working practices.

- Identify any possible improvements that could be made to improve sustainability.

Task four
Identify weaknesses and make recommendations for improvement

- Evaluate the system to identify significant weaknesses, which should be clearly explained along with their impact upon the organisation.

- For every weakness that has been identified, there should be one or more recommendations made to attempt to improve the situation.
  - The recommendations should concentrate on the effect that the changes would have on both the organisation and on individual members of staff. They may also highlight training needs or aids to improve staff performance, or changes needed to organisational culture.

- Prepare a cost-benefit analysis
  - At least one of the recommendations made should be subject to a cost-benefit analysis.
    Whilst not all benefits are quantifiable, all costs are, and students should make any necessary assumptions or 'guesstimates' to allocate costs to such items as time, unknown salaries, or any other unknown expense involved in the recommended changes.
  - All benefits should be identified, Including those that cannot be allocated a financial figure. This can include such things as improved customer relationships, improved documentation systems or staff morale (though this could be allocated a financial benefit as improving staff turnover cuts recruitment costs).

NOTE ON APPENDICES

Any charts and diagrams or supporting evidence should be included in an appendix and cross-referenced within the text. Any appendices included should be referred to in the main body of the report – or in the case of supporting statements to cover missing assessment criteria, mapped and cross-referenced to a copy of the unit standards.

COMPANY HISTORY

Cookridge & Cookridge Carpets Ltd is a large carpet, soft furnishings and bed dealership in Southampton. It is the main dealer for 'Memo@memory' foam beds and mattresses in the area, and has been trading for the past four years, having been established in 2009. It was set up by two brothers, Peter and John Cookridge.

Peter is a trained carpet fitter, and has been in the soft furnishing industry for the past twenty years. Before going into business with his brother he was the senior manager in a national carpet chain. His brother John, who is three years younger, was recently made redundant from his role as a mining engineer.

They decided to set up the business using John's £80,000 redundancy money and an inheritance the brothers received upon the death of their uncle. Peter only had a small mortgage on his house, and he managed to raise a loan of £100,000 (using the house as collateral) which was also invested in the business.

The brothers purchased a large plot of land on which they developed an aircraft hangar-sized building to use as the carpet and bed show room. They started out selling carpets, and then expanded into beds and soft furnishings. This expansion was organised by Peter, who had developed excellent working relationships with carpet manufacturers from his time in the industry.

In February 2013 Cookridge & Cookridge Carpets Ltd was asked by Memo Beds to become the main dealership for Southampton, as the existing local dealer was retiring and they wanted a local company to run their franchise. They have been very successful in direct sales, and have recently started selling carpets and beds over the internet. This venture seems to have increased business.

Peter is married to Sasha, who is a teacher in the local primary school for children with special needs. They have twin seventeen year-old boys, Mark and Matthew, who are both keen amateur rugby players and play for their local rugby club. Mark is at college studying for his 'A' levels, and Matthew has started a modern apprenticeship in motor engineering in a local garage which is run by a friend of his father. Peter's main hobby, besides watching his sons play rugby at the weekend, is building and racing motorbikes. He is a popular and well-known figure on the local motor racing scene.

John is married to Paula, who acted as company secretary for the first two years of the company's existence. She then left to have her first baby, who is now nine months old. Paula has now made the decision that she does not want to return to work, preferring to stay at home and be a full-time mother. The business employs twenty staff, composed of:

- nine direct sales people
- three internet sales staff
- two cleaners
- two car delivery drivers
- one accessories sales person
- three part-time staff in the small accounts department.

You have just been employed to work as the Senior Accounts Clerk, taking over most of Paula's old responsibilities. As the only full-time accounting staff member, you will supervise the running of the accounts office.

The carpet showroom's opening hours are as follows:

*   open seven days a week
*   operates from 09:00 until 21:00, Monday to Saturday
*   operates from 10:00 to 16:00 on Sunday.

The accounts department is open from 9am until 17.30pm, Monday to Friday.

The accounts department's office is located on the first floor of the showroom. Access to the office is by a set of stairs at the rear of the building. Toilet facilities for staff and customers are also on the first floor, so the stairs are used by members of the public.

Once on this floor, access to the accounts office is easy because the keypad lock is never used – the accounts staff prefer to keep the door propped open. The accounts office is open plan, with no private working areas.

Both the brothers are key holders for the building. They hold the only full sets of keys, as one of them is always on the premises at close of business to ensure the property is secure. There is an alarm code they set every evening when they lock up.

Accounts Department Staff

The current staff in the accounting office are:

*   **Sonja Douglas (Wages Clerk)**

    Sonja joined eight months ago. She is Paula's cousin, and joined the company when Paula decided she was not coming back to work. Although she is willing to work some extra hours if required, she does not want to commit herself to any more permanent hours as she would need to rearrange her child care. Sonja gained her qualification in payroll four years ago, but has not progressed any further since due to the arrival of her daughter Betty. She currently works full days on Wednesday and Thursday.

*   **Stefan Kalinowski (Accounts Clerk)**

    Stefan was employed one year ago. He works four days a week, and has chosen not to work on Fridays. This is because his main hobby is music, and he plays in a band every weekend; Friday is his rehearsal day. He has had no formal accounting training, but was trained on the job in his last role and by Paula before she left the company.

*   **Margaret Peterson (Accounts Clerk)**

    Margaret joined the company eighteen months ago (application letter on file, but no CV). She is employed on a part-time basis of five half days per week, and she likes to work these together to save on her bus fares to work. She currently works all day Tuesday and Wednesday, and a half-day on Thursday morning.

Note: the CVs and job descriptions that follow are also in Paula's personnel files.

CURRICULUM VITAE

Name	Sonja Douglas
Address	24 South Street
	SOUTHAMPTON
	S12 4RT
	Email: Sonja@btinternet.co.uk
	Mobile: 07792 236543
DOB	2 March 1984
Comments	As a working mother, I am a well organised and competent worker, dedicated to any role I take on.

Education

2004	AAT NVQ Level 2 in payroll gained at Southampton College
2002	A level maths, grade C
	A level general studies, grade A
2000	6 GCSEs at grade C and above including maths and English

Employment History

2004/5 Arthur C Clarke (engineering factory): trainee payroll clerk
2005/6 Arthur C Clarke: payroll clerk
Reason for leaving: pregnancy

2007/10 – Frescos: evening shelf stacker
Reason for leaving: to improve my career prospects now my daughter is in playschool

Hobbies	Swimming, playing with my baby daughter
References	Mr C Hancock, Managing Director, Arthur C Clarke & Co
	Mrs G Biggs, HR Manager, Frescos

JOB DESCRIPTION – WAGES CLERK

Hours	15 hours over two full days per week
Salary	To be agreed
Responsibilities	• To prepare weekly and monthly payroll information. To calculate all monies due (wages and commission) accurately.
	• To prepare payslips and make up pay packets for the weekly paid staff, and prepare BACS returns for monthly paid staff.
	• To prepare all associated returns and documentation.
	• Must be willing to undertake extra hours as needed.
Responsible to	The company secretary or office manager.
Responsible for	Self, security of information and security of payroll cash. As this is a new position, other duties may be required on an ad hoc basis.

CURRICULUM VITAE

Stefan Kalinowski
42 St James Avenue, Burnistly, Southampton, S25 6RE

DOB 30.5.1994

Overview
I left the sixth form of Burnistly Grammar School last year, as I wished to enter the world of work rather than go to university, and would like a career in accountancy. I am a bright, capable worker, and am happy to work on my own or as part of a team. I was Head Boy at school, and am happy to take on responsibility.

Last position

2012 - 2013	Accounts Receivable Clerk - Swanage County Supplies
	(Company went into administration and I was made redundant)

Education

2005 - 2012	Burnistly Grammar School
	GCSE Advanced levels - Accounting grade A
	Mathematics grade C
	Music grade A*

Aim To learn more about accounting and to become a qualified accountant.

Hobbies Music is a passion, both listening to it and playing. I play in a local group.

References

Mr J Johnson	Mrs C Smith
Accountant	Headteacher
Johnson & Co	Burnistly Grammar School
Eastborough	High Road
Swanage	Burnistly

JOB DESCRIPTION
Accounts Receivable Clerk (Sales Ledger)

Hours   37.5 hours over five days per week.

Responsibilities
- To prepare sales invoices
- To manage credit accounts
- To ensure that all payments are made within 90 days
- To prepare monthly management information
- Must be willing to undertake extra hours as needed

Responsible to   The company secretary or office manager.

Responsible for   Self, security of information and security of cash.

Margaret Peterson
10 Mandela Grove
Southampton
S2 4WS
30.6.2012

Dear Sir,

I wish to apply for the position of accounts clerk that was advertised in the Southampton Herald.

I am 57 years old and have recently been widowed. I need to return to work to supplement my income.

I have several years' experience in operating accounting systems, but have not worked in this area for over two years since I left my last role to care for my sick husband. However, though not qualified I am a competent accounts clerk and references can be obtained from my previous employer, with whom I worked for ten years.

Yours faithfully

M Peterson

M Peterson (Mrs)

JOB DESCRIPTION

Accounts Payable Clerk (Purchase Ledger)

Hours   20 hours over five days per week

Responsibilities
- To check GRN and purchase invoices
- To liaise with carpets, beds and soft furnishings suppliers
- To manage accounts payable accounts
- To ensure that all payments are made accurately and on time
- To prepare monthly management information
- Must be willing to undertake extra hours as needed

Responsible to   The company secretary or office manager

Responsible for   Self

COOKRIDGE & COOKRIDGE CARPETS (CCL LTD)

Mission Statement

Our mission is to provide an excellent level of service to all of our customers, whether they are spending £5 or £5000 – and to provide carpets, beds and soft furnishings that make a house into a home.

We are trying to be a greener company and we recycle wherever possible; we promise to remove all of the packaging from customers' premises, and dispose of this in an environmentally friendly way.

Information Technology Policy

All computers can only be accessed by staff who have been authorised by management to use Cookridge & Cookridge Carpets computers. All computers must be password protected.

Computers must only be loaded with licensed software owned by the company. No changes to software are permitted without consent of Cookridge & Cookridge Carpets' directors. No member of staff is allowed to load any software onto computers without prior permission from the management.

No unauthorised devices are to be used for saving, uploading or downloading work (e.g. discs, memory sticks, external hard drives or other devices) other than those purchased and approved by the company.

Computers should only be used for company business and must not be used to access any social networking site.

Staff making unfavourable comments regarding Cookridge & Cookridge Carpets, their management, operating procedures or customers on any social networking site will be deemed to be guilty of spoiling the reputation of the organisation and this will be a disciplinary matter.

Paula Cookridge
Company Secretary

INFORMATION TECHNOLOGY SYSTEMS

There are four computers in the office, as the brothers have provided one for every member of the accounts team.

These are all run on a standalone basis, though they are all linked to the same printer. The inventory information on beds, carpets and soft furnishings is kept on Microsoft Excel spreadsheets. Paula had worked with the software previously, and thought it would be a good idea to set up the company accounting system using the same software.

Three computers were purchased new when the company was established and are running on the Windows 7 operating system. They are also loaded with Microsoft Office 2010 (with a three user licence). Six months ago another new computer was purchased and loaded with Sage Payroll software to enable the payroll to be run in-house. The Microsoft Office package was also installed on this new computer.

When the computer system was set up a password was set to protect the information stored on it. The password is 'Paula C', and this is used for everything throughout the company because it was set up by Paula when she was company secretary and has never been changed. The idea was that the password would change every three months by having one keyword per computer and then changing the following number. For example, 'Slug1' would then change to 'Slug2' at the beginning of the next quarter, and three months later to 'Slug3', etc.

Paula had also asked everyone in the accounts office to give their computer a password and send it to her, so that she would be able to access all of the computers at any time. However, this was never done.

ACCOUNTS PAYABLE

Carpets and soft furnishings

All inventory is purchased on credit terms from a wide range of suppliers. This is one of Peter Cookridge's roles, and he enjoys spending time researching new inventory lines and new soft furnishing accessories; he also likes meeting the sales staff from different suppliers. He has a favourite group of suppliers he tends to use, mainly because they are sometimes willing to sponsor his motorbike building and racing efforts. There is no formal list of suppliers, and Peter keeps his own records.

All inventory levels are maintained on the Excel spreadsheets. These have been set up to show:
- suppliers
- cost prices
- selling prices
- profit margins
- re-order levels and quantities

Margaret has worked on Excel previously, but this was over two years ago. Whilst she is competent at inputting data, she sometimes struggles with anything beyond this.

Suppliers are paid at the end of the month that their invoice is received, as long as funds are available. However, since the recession some suppliers now request payment within thirty days of the date of invoice, and this is beginning to cause some concern.

Cookridge Carpets holds a large inventory, with many rolls of carpet in the warehouse for sale on a cash and carry basis. Peter has heard that some large companies have recently asked their suppliers to cut the wholesale price by 10%, and is considering approaching two of their largest suppliers to ask them whether this would be a possibility.

All suppliers are paid by cheque. These are completed by Margaret, and then signed by either John or Peter as they are now the only authorised signatories. The cheque book is stored in a locked desk drawer in Margaret's desk in the accounts office.

Memo Beds

Memo Beds supply all the memory foam beds to the organisation. These are now the bestselling line in beds. They supply products to Cookridge & Cookridge Carpets Ltd on a line of credit. The showroom beds are used as demonstration models, and these are paid for 90 days after receipt.

Customers' beds are purchased to order. A minimum deposit of 20% must be made when the order is placed and the rest of the monies are due for payment to the suppliers within 60 days.

Again, all inventory records are stored on Excel spreadsheets. It is the job of the warehouse manager to update the spreadsheets when inventory is delivered into the warehouse, or when inventory is moved from the warehouse into the showroom. This should always be supported by documented evidence, for example goods received notes (GRNs).

However, on busy days, the warehouse manager will often just update the spreadsheet when sending goods from the warehouse into the showroom, and then ask the sales staff for an inventory requisition note when they are less busy.

ACCOUNTS RECEIVABLE

Stefan is responsible for the running of this function. Whilst some customers do pay cash for their carpets, over 60% take extended credit terms. When Stefan first started at Cookridge & Cookridge Carpets, anyone who applied for a credit account was accepted.

However, Stefan realised that this was not good practice and he now uses a credit reference agency to ensure that potential new credit customers have no history of poor payments. Once they pass this check, any new customer who applies is automatically granted an unlimited line of credit.

All new credit accounts are set up on the first day of the month. Stefan often works extra hours on this day to ensure this task is completed. All sales orders are received by the showroom store staff for processing, and after completion are passed to the accounts department the next morning so that Stefan can prepare and record the invoices. Stefan has designed a form in Microsoft Word that he uses as a pro forma for invoicing.

To encourage sales, and to compete with large national retailers, Cookridge Carpets offers monthly payment terms to all customers with 6 months interest-free credit. Once this period expires there is an annual interest rate of 28.4%. They finance this through Westbridge Finance, which charges an annual rate of 8.7% to the company.

Stefan is responsible for ensuring payment occurs. The company policy regarding non-payment is as follows:

- Once payment is seven days overdue, Stefan will telephone the customer.
- If payment is not received within 14 days of the telephone call, then Stefan writes to the customer requesting payment and for the account to be brought into order.
- If payment is still not received within the next 14 days, the customer's details are passed onto a debt collection agency which works on behalf of the company.

The debt collection agency charges £80 per case, plus 30% of any monies collected. Though this is their policy, the Cookridge brothers think this is a very expensive option, and often do not bother following through with it.

CASH AND BANKING

Cash in

Stefan opens the mail every morning and sorts through it. Any cash or cheques received from customers are entered manually into a day book to record the receipt. The day book is then used to update the ledger accounts, and the cheques and cash are placed in the office safe until a banking day.

At the end of every day, all cash and cheques are removed from the tills, leaving a float of £100 cash in each for the start of the next day. The principle is that the till should be balanced to ensure that the cash content is correct.

However, during the week this does not happen as the store closes at 21:00, and the sales staff feel that they should not be asked to do an extra job at this hour.

As a result, it is common practice that all cash (except for the till floats) and cheques are removed and bagged as takings from individual tills, before being stored in the safe in the accounts office.

Banking

Banking is carried out on a Monday and Thursday, and this is normally Stefan's job that he does during his lunch break.

There is often less cash banked on Thursdays. This is because John and Peter have started to take available cash from the office safe to pay wages, in order to reduce the amount of money drawn from the bank using cheques.

Authorised signatories

Any one signature from:

- Peter Cookridge
- John Cookridge
- Paula Cookridge (removed from mandate 30.10.13)

Petty cash

£100 is drawn from the bank every month and placed in a tin. A list of what it is used for is kept in a notebook in the tin, and anyone using the petty cash money is expected to make a note of the date and expense, and sign against this. The tin is kept in the staff room, next to the coffee and tea.

WAGES AND SALARIES

Until six months ago, the payroll was completed by the company's accountants, Southampton Accounting Services. Initially Paula was going to run the payroll, but found that this was too demanding of her time and so she decided to commission the accountants to perform this task.

However, because the individual hours worked each week by staff (and commissions earned on carpet sales) are so variable, the payroll run is different every week. The accountants charged for the time taken to complete the payroll, so it became a costly process for the company.

The brothers decided that wages and salaries could be run internally. For the first two months they used a temping agency, but this was also an expensive option. When Sonja started working for the company eight months ago, she took over payroll duties.

All staff except those in the accounts department are paid weekly in cash. Pay packets are available from the showroom manager, Jim Andrews, from 10:00 on a Friday morning. The rest of the staff are paid monthly, by cheque, on the last working day of each month.

The following table sets out the working hours, rates of pay and frequency of payments for the various categories of staff in the company.

Staff	Rate	Normal time	Time and a half	Double time	Pay period
Sales	£8 per hour	40 hours	Hours over 42 Monday to Saturday	Sunday hours	Weekly
Showroom Manager	£9.50 per hour	40 hours	Hours over 42 Monday to Saturday	Sunday hours	Monthly
General staff	£7 per hour	40 hours	Hours over 42 Monday to Saturday	Sunday hours	Weekly
Accounts	£16,000 pro-rata	37.5 hours per week	None - salaried	None - salaried	Monthly

Sales staff earn a commission of 2% on the first £30,000 of sales per month, and 5% on any sales over that figure.

John Cookridge is responsible for preparing staff rotas to ensure that there is adequate staff coverage for all of the opening hours. Most of the sales staff are willing to work overtime, so this does not usually create any problems.

Once the week has finished, the completed rotas are given to Sonja who uses them to calculate the amount of hours that the individual staff have worked.

Sonja prepares the payslips from this information on a Wednesday, calculating manually any overtime or Sunday working payments due. She then calculates how much cash needs to be drawn from the bank and uses the company cheque book (which is kept locked in Margaret's desk) to prepare a cheque ready for signing.

On a Thursday she prepares the pay packets, which are stored in the office safe for the showroom manager to collect and hand out the following day, though often any member of the sales staff who is not busy will actually do this. Any pay packets not given out are returned to the office safe and remain there until collected by the relevant member of staff.

Salaried staff are paid monthly on the last working day of the month, and this is done using the Bankers Automated Clearing Services (BACS). The BACS information is prepared by the wages clerk, signed by either of the brothers, and needs to be with the bank by 25th of every month.

Envelopes with payslips are handed to each member of the salaried staff by Sonja on the day they are paid. If a staff member is not available, the envelope is placed in their desk drawer. There are no adjustments to be made to any of the monthly paid staff, as overtime payments are not made to them.

Statutory Sick Pay (SSP) is paid to the showroom staff, but office staff are salaried and are allowed six weeks contractual sick pay per year.

The brothers have always trusted their workforce completely, and there is no requirement or system in place for either sales or office employees to sign in or out when they start or finish work.

DIARY OF EVENTS

August 2012

Peter had taken Wednesday off to take Mark up to London to a university open day. Mark had just finished college, and was going to have that week off before starting as a temporary staff member in the showroom so that he could learn the family business, even though he was more interested in trying to become a full-time rugby player.

Sonja was standing by the printer, complaining that yet again the payslips had jammed the mechanism. She was annoyed because the payslips had to be purchased from Sage, and not only were they very expensive, but she only had enough left for this week and next week's payroll run, and she did not want to have to reorder more before she went on holiday.

When Sonja recovered the payslips from the printer, she realised that half of them were now unusable, and so would have to be destroyed. After dropping them in the bin, she asked Stefan to order more before she reprinted the weekly wages run.

Sonja thought it was just bad luck when a message appeared on her computer to show that the printer ink cartridge needed to be replaced. She was further annoyed because she had asked Stefan to replace this yesterday when he was printing out the invoices, but he had failed to do this. She threw the empty cartridge in the bin before reminding Stefan that it was only fair for him to change the ink when he saw that it was low. All Sonja wanted was for the day to finish as she was really annoyed with Stefan, and nothing had gone right for her.

Stefan's music was his main love outside of his work. Whilst he was happy to work longer hours than the other accounting staff, he wanted to keep his Fridays free for music. Peter could see no problem with this, so Stefan now worked flexi-time, arriving an hour before any of the other accounting staff and departing an hour later to make up his hours so that he did not have to work on Fridays.

As Stefan was the first one in the building on Monday morning, he was opening the post and logging cash and cheques that had arrived into the day book, when the telephone rang. It was Margaret to say that she had suffered from very bad toothache over the weekend, and had an emergency dental appointment for that morning so she would be late for work. Stefan went back to his task of opening the mail, without noticing he had dropped a cheque he was just about to write into the day book behind the desk.

Paula called into the office to show off her baby before she joined John for a family lunch. As she was short on cash and did not have time to go to the bank, she helped herself to £40 from the petty cash tin, and told Stefan that John would replace it this afternoon when he returned from their lunch date.

John was becoming concerned that some customers were becoming increasingly slow in making payments on their credit accounts. He asked Stefan to prepare a schedule of debtors, but Stefan was busy doing invoices and asked if this could be done next month. Stefan had not chased up late payments recently because Paula had said that although she was meant to do this on a weekly basis, she only did it when she had time.

September 2012

Sonja was going on holiday this month. The last time she went on holiday, she completed two weeks of pay packets on the same date (all based on the hours worked in the week prior to her preparing the wage packets) because she knew that she was the only member of staff who could operate the Sage payroll system. She completed these pay packets and placed them in the safe, informing her supervisors that Stefan would give them out each Friday, and that any over- or under-payments would be adjusted in the following week after she returned to work.

However, there had been mistakes in this process, and it had taken a full month for the resulting errors to be corrected so Peter had said that she should not do this again. This time, Sonja asked Margaret if she could do the wages run for the weeks of her absence, because she knew that many years ago Margaret used to operate a payroll. Margaret promised her she would try and do this, but she did not know how to operate Sage. Instead, Margaret said she could prepare the payroll manually using HMRC tax and NI tables, and then Sonja could update the computer system when she came back from holiday.

It was a hot Monday morning and the sales staff complained to Jim Andrews that the milk had gone sour in the refrigerator and they could not have any drinks because of this. Jim sent Kim Lee, a junior member of the sales staff, to go to the nearby store and buy 2 litres of milk, telling her to take the money out of the petty cash tin. She returned saying there was no money left in the tin, and so Jim took £10 out of the till and put a note in saying what he had done. When Jim complained to Margaret, she said it was strange because there had been £100 put into the tin a week before, and yet on checking the note book there was only £40 spent in the last two weeks.

On the second Tuesday of the month, the bank telephoned to warn the company that as they had reached their overdraft limit they were unable to honour a direct debit due out that day. John said that this was just an oversight and he would deal with it immediately. He emptied the tills and banked £900 in cash so that the direct debit would be covered. He then asked Stefan to produce an aged receivables list so that he could see why the cash flow was so limited when trade had appeared to have picked up. John was disappointed to note that Stefan had not been chasing up debts owed beyond an initial phone call if the debtor stated that they would ensure the payments were brought up to date.

Mark was helping Stefan in the office as part of his summer job. Stefan was busy updating invoices, and thinking that Mark had read all the company policies, he let Mark open two new credit accounts for customers. Mark did this, but without taking any credit references.

On returning from holiday, Sonja was approached by Jo Sellers, one of the sales team. He had been expecting commission totalling £80 in his wages, but Margaret had not allowed for this and had only prepared his wages based on basic hours worked. He told Sonja that he really needed this money, but Sonja knew she could do nothing about this until the next wages run, and told him so.

Jo was so upset by this that Sonja told him she would borrow the money out of the petty cash tin and replace it when she made his wages up. He was very pleased, and told her that she had made his day, as he had to buy a birthday present for his mother. Sonja was pleased to have helped him, but made a mental note to ask Peter or John if they could provide some training for Margaret so that she could work out the commissions due.

October 2012

A new warehouse manager, Joe Bloggins, was employed this month. His last job was at a well-known DIY store, where he was the deputy warehouse manager. The first task he did was to complete an inventory check, and he informed the brothers that there was a shortfall of £3,000 in the actual physical inventory against that on record. He complained to the brothers that there was no evidence of when goods had been taken from the warehouse to the showroom.

Joe also noted that the company they were using to remove the waste cardboard and paper were charging per collection, and had started to collect on a weekly basis rather than twice a month as contracted. When he pointed this out to the waste collection service, they informed him that the previous warehouse manager had asked for this increase because there was so much packaging to collect. This had been done without informing the management, whom he knew would be happy to accept this as it was an environmental issue. Joe thought that the brothers should contact the new employer of the previous warehouse manager to inform them that he should have been given a written warning after making contractual changes without the required authorisation.

Stefan went to John to inform him that there was a major supplier account due to be paid and that the overdraft limit would not allow them to draw this cheque. Stefan had checked the invoice, as it was for nearly three times greater than was normal from this supplier, but all seemed to be in order. John did not know why this had happened, but when he asked Peter why he had placed such a large order, Peter informed him that the supplier had promised to sponsor his next motorcycle show if he increased his order.

Peter thought that this would be good business practice and would help increase trade. When John told him that this supplier could not be paid due to poor cash flow, Peter was very annoyed as he did not want to lose the sponsorship. After having an argument over the amount that had been ordered, John then agreed to telephone the bank and explain the situation, and to ask them for an increased overdraft limit for one month only to allow the supplier to be paid.

November 2012

Once again Sonja was complaining that the printer was jammed with payslips, which had meant her throwing away the spoilt payslips for the monthly paid staff. She asked Peter if they could have a new printer, or just print the payslips on plain paper, as she did not have the time to align the printer and the payslips correctly.

Joe is also a motorbike fanatic, and on the first weekend of the month he went to a motorbike rally with Peter. Whilst there, he told Peter he was settling in well, but was unhappy with the record keeping system for inventory control. Another error had occurred recently when one of the warehouse staff had entered a delivery incorrectly onto the spreadsheet whilst Joe was on his lunch break. Peter said that as Christmas was approaching they would be very busy, but after Christmas he would review the matter with John and Joe together. The conversation then reverted to the Christmas party, and the subject was not raised again.

Joe Bloggins spoke to Sonja and explained that he had taken on an extra member of staff for the Christmas rush and January sales. He said that the new member would be paid on an hourly rate, and that as he was a student he would not pay tax, and would just need a cash payment weekly. Sonja asked for the new starter document that all new employees had to complete, but Joe had not asked for this to be done, and instead asked Sonja to just add him to the payroll system and he would send through the completed document later on. Sonja agreed, and added new worker A. Lias to the payroll, leaving herself a diary note to ask Joe for the documentation.

December 2012

The first weekend was the office Christmas party which was held at the Grand Hotel. They had a great time, especially since the brothers had agreed to pay for the evening and had given everyone a £10 allowance for drinks.

Stefan's brother, Adalbert (known as Addie for short) was home from university for the Christmas holidays. Trade was beginning to increase, and January sales were looming. Stefan had mentioned how busy the showroom staff were, and so Addie asked Peter if there were any holiday jobs available, as he could use the extra money to help fund his next year at university. Peter was happy to employ him for the next six weeks – not in the showroom, but in the warehouse.

It was Stefan's role to prepare invoices and send them to customers. He gathered the information by completing day books from the purchase orders which were written out by the sales staff in the showroom. As Stefan did not work on a Friday, he was always very busy on Monday, as he had invoices from both Friday and Saturday to prepare. However, now that Addie was working, Stefan came up with the idea that Addie could write up the day books from the purchase orders, and this would save him time on a Monday morning.

Addie was also into music, and as he had been working on a voluntary project whilst at university he discussed with Stefan the possibility of doing some type of community event, based on music, to enhance the lives of the children at the nearby school for children with severe learning disabilities (where Sasha worked). Whilst Peter thought that this was a good idea, John was not too happy about it, and said that if they wanted to do this they would need to arrange it in their own time, and use their holiday entitlement days for it.

Stefan asked Peter and John if he could start college next month to further his AAT studies on a part-time basis. Both of the brothers thought that this would be a good idea, and said that whilst they could not give him any time off to study, they were willing to pay the cost of his course, books and exam fees as long as he guaranteed that he would continue to work for them for one year after completing his course. Stefan was very happy to do this and signed an agreement to this fact. Peter and John were discussing the importance of training and though they felt that Margaret was probably too old to benefit from this, they decided to offer Sonja training as well, with the same conditions. Sonja was not willing to sign an agreement tying her to the company and said she knew her job, and did not need any more training.

Knowing that they were trying to keep receivables accounts more in line with their agreed credit terms, Stefan asked Mark to telephone all customers with overdue outstanding balances. One customer, A. Smith and Jones Ltd, stated that they had paid their account in full by cheque over six weeks ago and were very annoyed that they were now being chased for money.

CarPet Supplies, one of their major suppliers, have requested urgent payment of an invoice that has been outstanding for 60 days. This invoice was for £30,000 and though this would normally have been paid there were not enough funds in the bank to cover this amount. When Margaret informed John of this, he was very surprised at the amount of the invoice, and asked her to review all the goods received notes (GRNs) for May to see what carpets had been ordered to cause such a large invoice. Margaret spent a day completing this reconciliation and found that there was an error and they had been charged for 1,000 metres of twisted Wilton instead of 100, this having a wholesale price of £16.99 per metre plus VAT.

January 2013

Paula came to the office on a Tuesday. Her sister had taken the baby out for the day so she had some free time on her hands. The office was busy as Sonja was on holiday, and Paula was happy to help out by answering the telephone and writing some letters. Paula had just made a coffee and came back to Margaret's desk, which is where she was working, when the phone rang. The caller identified himself as John Commins, the boyfriend of Angel, one of the sales staff. He asked to speak to her, but when Paula checked she discovered that Angel was on holiday that week. John said it was urgent that he spoke with her so Paula gave him Angel's home telephone number and address from Sonja's personnel files.

The bill for the Christmas party was received from the Grand Hotel. It averaged out at £160 per head, including all the drinks and wine. John asked Margaret to put the bill through the company accounts by splitting the bill so that £140 was put through as a tax-deductible expense, and the other £20 per head put through as a subsistence claim against expenses. However, Margaret knew the bill came to £160 per head, and that as such it was over the limit of £150 as a legitimate taxable expense, and therefore should not be included. Whilst Margaret was aware that the method John was asking her to use to account for this bill would mean a smaller tax liability, she did not like to do this because it was in breach of current HMRC rules. She did account for the bill by splitting it because she was frightened of what John would say if she did not comply with his wishes.

Peter and John were discussing the possibility of expanding and opening a new showroom in Brighton, about seventy miles away from their current location. They felt that they could run this by just employing one member of staff, managing the new showroom themselves to start with by travelling on a daily basis, and even by asking some of their staff in Southampton to travel across to help out if the Brighton shop got busy. They realised that if they were to do this, they would need to look at the finance options open to them, as they would need to borrow heavily to capitalise this venture.

Peter was very concerned as although trade had picked up throughout the summer, they were still not trading at the same level as they had been last year. John reassured him, saying that by having two branches trade must increase, and that the only problem was that the accounts for this year would not show such a healthy financial position. However, the company only prepared accounts on an annual basis, and had only ever needed to produce these for HMRC, and therefore he could not prove how this year's trading was actually going. He then suggested that the way to maximise their chances of obtaining the required bank borrowing would be to ask Paula to step in and prepare up to date accounts that showed the company in the best possible light by reducing the amount of monies owed to creditors for accounts payable.

Stefan was annoyed when he discovered that one of the credit accounts that Mark had opened for I Khan had made no payments against credit given at all so far. This customer had bought £1000 worth of goods and paid an initial deposit in July but had made no payment since then. When Stefan tracked back through the account he realised that no credit reference agency had been used, so he decided to contact the agency to check on this customer, only to find that he had a very poor credit score.

Addie was due to return to university next month. As his printer was not working at home, and he wanted to download and print his timetables, reading list and course information, he came to the office one evening when he knew Stefan would be on his own to use the printer in the accounts office. Peter was therefore surprised when he walked into the office after returning from a meeting with a supplier to find Addie sat alone at Sonja's computer, using both the computer and printer. When he asked where Stefan was, Addie replied he had gone into the warehouse because there was a problem with the physical inventory balance not matching up with that on the spreadsheet records.

Mark was tidying up in the office one evening as he waited for his father to come and pick him up. All the staff had gone for the evening, but Peter had promised his son a lift home. He decided to rearrange the furniture and was surprised to discover two cheques behind a desk. One was dated August, and one November. He gave them to his father, who said he did not know where they came from but would bank them the next day.

February 2013

Mark had decided not to go to university but to enter the family business instead. He decided he was going to work in all areas of the business to gain a full understanding of what was happening, and he would particularly like to look at the purchasing of inventory as he felt that this could be managed better.

All the temporary staff were now laid off, and Sonja realised that she still had no information regarding A. Lias, the temporary warehouse worker who Joe Bloggins had employed. She tried ringing the mobile phone number Joe had given her for him, but found the number was unobtainable.

Once again the company had reached its overdraft limit and the wages needed to be paid. Stefan and Mark started to telephone customers with the largest outstanding overdue balances. When ringing one customer; Mr Smythe in South Havant, Mark was surprised when he said he had dropped £500 in cash into the store four weeks ago. Mr Smythe said he had given it to one of the sales staff, and noted that this was a young man, with curly hair, a description which fitted one of the newer sales staff members. Mark went into the store to ask the manager about this cash, and the manager informed him that he knew nothing about it but would make some enquiries. He then organised a search in the store and three hours later called Mark to say that the money had been found in an envelope with Mr Smythe's name on it in the back of a drawer, but that no one could recall it being handed in to them.

Margaret noticed that there was no petty cash left and they needed some money to buy toilet rolls. Peter took £100 out of his pocket and added it to the tin, as that was all the cash he had with him, but again noted there were no entries in the petty cash book, just several IOUs in the tin.

John and Peter informed the staff that they would be away for the third week in February, as they were going on a family holiday to celebrate their parents' golden wedding anniversary. Peter was concerned that they would be leaving the staff without any financial resources, so he and John both signed a cheque book containing 30 blank cheques so that any bills could be paid if necessary. They gave this into the care of Margaret who placed it in the top drawer of her desk, and promised it would only be used if necessary.

During this week Jo Sellers came to Sonja and explained that once again the commission he had received was not what he had expected, and he was £65 down. He said he needed this to pay his rent. Sonja didn't think that any mistake had been made, but she said that once again she would advance him this, as long as it was repaid from his next commission payment. However, when she went to the petty cash tin, this was empty. She knew, however, that Margaret had a supply of signed blank cheques, so she used one of these making it out to cash, and went to the bank to withdraw £100 for petty cash, ensuring she noted the advance to Jo in the petty cash book.

Index

for your notes

for your notes

for your notes

for your notes

for your notes

for your notes